To Our Grandchildren
Mark
Kyrsten
Jordan
Curtis
Nathan
Beloved by their grandparents
as though there were no

CONTENTS

PREFACE

This book describes Christian marriage and tells how some of the common problems in husband-and-wife relationships may be resolved. Christian marriage is an ideal in the mind of God, made practical by the application of appropriate biblical patterns which permit creative approaches to family interests and needs.

Not all married Christians practice Christian marriage. One of the purposes of this book is to stimulate husbands and wives to make their marriages both creative and Christian. This we partly achieve through viewing marriage and the family from the biblical point of view, through practicing individual faith, cultivating mutuality, managing money, understanding sexual intimacy, and maturing in marriage. There is not enough space for an exhaustive treatment of these topics or for introducing all the issues related to creative Christian marriage.

Many books have been published during recent years for the purpose of assisting family development. The growing demand for family conferences, religious and secular, has given rise to an increasing number of speakers specializing in marriage themes. During a recent calendar year I spoke to 27 family or couples conferences. But a decade earlier I did not hold one family conference during an entire year, although the year was a busy one for other themes.

In evangelical church circles family life did not appear to be threatened until the midpoint of the 1960s. Circumstances have changed dramatically. Home and family problems are serious and grievous. Christian churches and other religious organizations have inaugurated programs, established counseling centers, and sponsored conferences to help meet the current problems related to troubled families. Concern about this led to the first major conference on Christian family renewal sponsored by evangelicals. It was held in St. Louis in the fall of 1975, and more than 2,000 Christian leaders attended.

This book is a selection and adaptation of addresses delivered in family conferences and seminars in the United States and Canada. It is a companion volume to *Our Children Are Our Best Friends* (paperback edition, *Our Children: Our Best Friends*), published by Zondervan Publishing Company. Virtually all illustrations are from experiences of Christians with whom I have counseled. In some instances details have been camouflaged to protect the privacy of those persons involved, but the substance of each case history has been retained.

These chapters presuppose a knowledge of the Christian Scriptures by readers. The biblical texts are important, and some of the development of thought is dependent upon knowledge of the passages referred to at the beginning of each chapter. In some chapters the biblical passage is not directly utilized in the text; however, it is hoped that nothing in this book is contrary to any biblical principle. It is also hoped that each reader will discover his own creative ideas based on scriptural insights.

Perhaps all authors feel that they can find no satisfactory way to express appreciation to those who have encouraged and helped them in their writing. Nearly all of them acknowledge their debt in a few words at the beginning of a writing and hope that the statements will be read and believed. With that same faith, I express profound gratitude and love to my wife, who is constant, who listens to me, reads my manuscripts and generously permits our experiences to be used in the hope that they will benefit others.

My gratitude is expressed also to my secretary, Yvonne Cederblom, for repeatedly typing each chapter to accommodate my editings. She must have mastered the material!

My appreciation is extended to the trustees of Simpson College, who provide me with freedom to follow the course of ministry that I believe to be God's will for my life. Their backing, together with that of the faculty, staff and students, makes possible the achievement of several of my personal goals. With that volume of support, any failure in this venture must be entirely my own.

PART ONE

MARRIAGE

This is a great mystery: but I speak concerning Christ and the church. (Eph. 5:32)

CHAPTER ONE

A CREATIVE ACT

Key points in this chapter include:
- why traditional marriage receives a bad press
- why traditional marriage is alive and well
- what really started with Adam and Eve
- why cohabitation is neither new nor unusual
- what weaknesses emerge in "living together arrangements"
- what the marriage license means in society

Male and female created he them; and blessed
them, and called their name Adam, in the day
when they were created. (Gen. 5:2, *KJV*)

For there are different reasons why men cannot marry: some, because they were born that
way; others, because men made them that
way; and others do not marry because of the
Kingdom of heaven. Let him who can do it
accept this teaching. (Matt. 19:12, *TEV*)

If the media reflects society there is a decline of belief
in traditional marriage. Critics prophesy its ultimate ex-
tinction. However, these popular reports are overstated
and given too much credence. Even skeptical news re-
porters have begun to reproduce statistics that show
marriage is not as out of date as debunkers assert.[1]
Emerging evidence suggests that old values have not
totally decayed. And some evidence even suggests a
recovery of that which has been lost.

It is well known that the media thrive on stories ac-
centing deviations from the norm. Marriage has been
subject to reporting that accents the bizarre and any
revolt against old values. The facts are distorted in the
process. Will and Ariel Durant write: "We must remind
ourselves again that history as usually written ... is
quite different from history as usually lived: the histori-
an records the exceptional because it is interesting—
because it is exceptional. . . . Behind the red facade of
war and politics, misfortune and poverty, adultery and
divorce, murder and suicide, were millions of orderly
homes, devoted marriages, men and women kindly and
affectionate, ..."[2]

The press portrays an entertainment figure as an authority on love, marriage and freedom. Yet that celebrity may hold a dismal personal record of marriage failure. Historians will likely poke fun at the twentieth century for its choices of heroes. It is incredible that the general population can be manipulated into believing pronouncements on life by failures, misfits, novices, troubled and disillusioned persons.

The public appears to be titillated by gossip about the intimacies of public men and women. To be discreet or private about sin is seen as hypocrisy. But society might do well to cultivate such "hypocrisy" in order to protect impressionable youths during their development.

In the confusion of these mixed reviews of modern marriage, the Christian marital pattern stands out as timelessly effective and satisfying. It is not to be approached with a nostalgic longing for the traditions of the past. Rather, it is to be seen as an ideal to be reached for, an ideal that exists in the mind of God. That ideal is revealed in the Scripture and observed in the models of many Christian marriages.

Adam and Eve—Two as One

God created Adam and Eve to function as one: "The twain shall be one flesh." The unity underlies the use of the word "man" to refer either to Adam or to Adam and Eve together (Gen. 5:2). This use of language was not designed to exhibit male egotism. Rather, the one-flesh unity of man and woman makes it appropriate to signify the human race as "man." The word stands for a part as well as the whole. Part of man is male (man) and part is female (woman). Sexual division is important only after the race of man has been identified. All human beings comprise the race of man. In English usage context clearly indicates when "man" means "race" and when it means "male."

13

When Adam and Eve acted independently of each other, trouble entered their partnership and alienated them from God. The war between the sexes perpetuates the tragic drive for independence which was one of the causes of the banishment of man (male and female) from Eden. In the beginning male and female were at one in virtually every dimension. That first unity is the biblical ideal. Every married couple should have as a major goal the recovery of that primal unity.

God's creative act in marriage has not been superseded. No substitute has been found for it. Current attacks on it will not succeed. Marriage seems to have lost some recent battles in the social conflict. Such battles recur from century to century. Each time the eventual victory has gone to marriage. Our contention is that it always will.

All societies recognize the creative and unifying aspects of marriage. The sexual act itself combines these two apects. It is an act that physically unifies two partners, and it is the means by which procreation is achieved. Through marriage male and female are to do what God did. God created. Man procreates. Each child is a repetition of what God did in the Garden of Eden. That is one of the important reasons why the Bible has so much to say about marriage and its spiritual significance. It is important, then, that marriage be maintained in a profoundly spiritual context.

It is obvious that sexual intercourse is the physical symbol of the spiritual unity between a man and a woman. The Bible states that the sexual act makes the two participants one. Therefore, asserted Jesus, the joining of a man with a harlot is to be understood as an act which has the quality of marriage. The union of two persons spiritually is illustrated in the physical union. Participation in the physical union without this understanding suggests that sexual partners are manipulating one another as objects. Elements of exploitation are present and the act is robbed of the greatness of its purpose.

"Just Living Together" Is Nothing New

A major modern challenge to the biblical marriage pattern is the increasing acceptance of couples living together without being married. Numerous popular articles discuss the subject. These articles create the impression that cohabitation without marriage is an exciting new development. As a matter of fact, it is an ancient practice, as the history of "common-law" marriages demonstrate.

In 1877 the United States Supreme Court ruled that "common-marriages are valid unless the state in question has a specific law which declares them to be illegal." Since then more than two-thirds of the states have passed laws prohibiting common-law marriage.[3] These laws were believed to be a move away from a socially unhealthy practice.

It appears that during the early twentieth century there was a decline in the number of couples living together without marriage. This was probably because legal benefits had increased for married women and their children. But, during the third quarter of the century a marked rise in cohabitation occurred. The unusual feature of this resurgence was the willingness of cohabiting unmarrieds to openly acknowledge living together without official ceremony. Openly living together began to be seen as a badge of courage, and it was alleged to be superior to traditional marriage.

Through the media, the general society was urged to believe that traditional virtue was unrealistic, nonexistent, or even wrong. Persons who maintained and defended Christian values and marital fidelity were often labeled "square" and "naive." The derision was effective in persuading many young people to turn away from traditional marriage. The Evidence of the frequent failure of intimate relationships without marriage was generally ignored.

Throughout history one of the reasons couples lived together without marriage has been a desire to avoid the commitment and responsibility of traditional marriage. Not willing to become trapped by lifelong family responsibilities, they tried to tailor their relationships to their convenience. Since they felt incapable of successful marriage for themselves, they tended to blame the institution of marriage itself.

Other factors made it possible to avoid marriage. Homosexuality and prostitution were commonplace in the ancient world, as they are in nearly every nation during our time. The great example of love discussed by Plato in *The Phaedrus* was a story of a man and a lad in a homosexual experience. Socrates, with all his wisdom, suffered marital discord and was accused of sexual deviation. Gibbon's eminent book about Rome shows that the progressive weakening of the family was a leading cause of the empire's decline.[4] Birth control was effectively practiced in later Rome by the expedient of men resorting to prostitution to meet their sexual needs. A leading industry in ancient Corinth for a lengthy period was prostitution. The remnants of "the oldest profession in the world" remained to plague the Christians in Corinth to whom the apostle Paul wrote.

Though deviations from marriage and fidelity have been present throughout history, they have not won the day. No nation has survived the collapse of marriage. That which God has created, man will not put asunder.

Modern couples living together outside of marriage

often advocate the human need for deep personal commitment. But they reject by their conduct the greatest possible commitment of man and woman in marriage. To live together without marriage is to imply that one or both members of the liaison are not willing to make the commitment called for. They point out that their commitment of love is unsullied by meddlesome governmental regulations and outmoded religious traditions. But their claims are not matched by practice. The average length of these "total commitments" is seven months. The hard evidence of these relationships shows that they are transient and they are in truth ineffective arguments against contracted marriage.

It is common to hear from couples that they have not married because they do not want to go through the "paper work." This is a clever line, but hardly a reason to avoid marriage. One young woman approached me following an address in which the issue of liaison without marriage was challenged and criticized. She said, "I'm just living with my guy. We have an apartment and are doing fine. We are committed to each other."

Two young persons close by listened to her with admiring approval. I replied, "Then why not get married and declare by that act to the whole society that you are committed to each other?"

"Too much paper work," she replied, taking on a pseudo-sophisticated air. "We are not held by a piece of paper."

I shifted the subject somewhat to divert her attention. Shortly I asked if she had a pet. She acknowledged that she had a pet dog. I inquired if the dog was loved by her.

"Yes."

"Do you have a license for the dog?" I asked.

"Yes," she answered, "we have to license the dog in this state."

"Where did you get it?"

"At the fire station. We get licenses at the fire station in this state."

"How did you get the license?"

"Went down and signed for it."

"That interests me," I replied. "You care enough for the dog to do the paper work, but you don't care that much for your 'guy.'"

The young persons listening to the exchange silently turned and walked away. I pointed to my wife standing in the corner of the room and said to the young woman, "I loved her enough 30 years ago to contract marriage. I promised to be loyal to her when I would not feel as loving as I did on our wedding day. I wanted to protect my wife during times when I would feel unloving or unwilling to do my duty. And those times did arise."

The conversation ended. The girl turned away, solemn and thoughtful.

Without the legal obligation of a marriage certificate I might have lost, through abandonment in a weak moment, that human relationship which has become the most significant treasure of my life. At a conference I once asked, "How many of you men would have at some time in your experience walked away from your marriage had you not been obligated by a contract?" Nearly every man lifted a hand. Raising the same question with the wives of those men, my wife received a similar response. Casual liaisons do not have the benefit of a marriage license to carry the couple through what ought to be transitory human and marital problems.

Reference has already been made to common-law marriage in the early decades of this century. A man and woman were presumed to be legally married if they lived together for a period of time. Society requires an orderly system to provide justice in the protection of citizens, equity in the payment of taxes, fairness in the division of property, and the like. It was found to be nearly impossible to provide such services apart from legally recognized family units.

New tries are being made at protecting rights of persons who cohabit without marriage. The greatest losses appear to be the children born to unwed parents. Order and justice have required states to legalize, or treat as legal, the "families" who were not licensed, or else to deny privileges and rights to persons who flaunt the established system.

The excessive number of persons from common-law marriage appearing on welfare rolls and as wards of the state provides sufficient evidence to deny the alleged superiority of cohabitation without marriage. If marriage were to end as a legal institution, society would not possess the mechanism or resources to care for its children. Or the number of children might decline so severely as to weaken the nation.

Cohabiting couples experience all the problems of marrieds. They may even turn to marriage counselors for help in intimate relationships. Unmarried couples make up 20 percent of the cases brought to the Center for Behavior Therapy in California. But success in dealing with their problems is disappointing. Dr. Donald F. Cowan said, "Unmarried couples who seek help often don't have the commitment to each other to follow through with therapy."[5] Jarle Brors, founder of the Institute of Marriage and Family Relations in Washington, writes: "The understanding when they live together is that they are free. . . . But it doesn't really work that way. It's not much different from marriage except that in one case they have a ring and in one they don't."[6] But that ring is an important difference.

The evidence of failure in casual liaisons has not been

made clear to the public. As a result, the apparent ease with which casual liaisons are made and broken has had a detrimental effect upon marriage solidarity. Because of fanciful claims of excitement among cohabiting couples, the partners in a marriage are sometimes influenced to make less of their own commitment than they might otherwise have done. They feel that they have missed an elusive excitement. Instead of revitalizing their marriages, they separate. Divorce, once a sin in society, is now seen as an acceptable option.

The point made here is that marriage is a creative act of God. Alternative proposals to marriage have been unsuccessful in aggregate, therefore unconvincing as substitutes. Since marriage is of God, given in the time of man's innocency and maintained throughout history, it will not be dissolved through cultural revolution. Neither the problems of marriage nor attacks on it will destroy the institution. And for Christians the spiritual meaning of marriage creates even greater confidence in its solidarity.

Notes

1. *Times-Delta*, Visalia, California, October 13, 1972. (The article is a summary of a survey sponsored by *Better Homes and Gardens* and reported under the title, "What's Happening to the American Family?") *San Francisco Chronicle*, July 10, 1973. "Two to One Odds Make Marriage a Good Bet." *The Reader's Digest*, January 1973, p. 106ff, and February 1973, p. 111ff. *Time*, July 9, 1973, p. 64.
2. Will and Ariel Durant, *The Lessons of History* (New York: Simon & Schuster, 1968), p. 41.
3. Gary Collins, Editor, *Make More of Your Marriage*. John Scanzoni, "Christian Perspective on Alternative Styles of Marriage" (Waco, Texas: Word Publishing Co., 1976), p. 160.
4. Gibbon, *The Rise and Fall of the Roman Empire*.
5. Ann Blackman, "When Unweds Break Up," *San Francisco Examiner*, September 19, 1972., p. 11.
6. Ibid.

CHAPTER TWO

A CHRISTIAN ANALOGY

Key points in this chapter include:
- how Christian marriage is an analogy of Christ and His church
- what Paul thought about women and equality between the sexes
- how marriage partners are equal but hold different roles
- how marriage portrays Christian growth
- why Christian marriage is possible

Submitting yourselves one to another in the fear of God. Wives, submit yourselves unto your own husbands, as unto the Lord. For the husband is the head of the wife, even as Christ is the head of the church: and he is the saviour of the body. Therefore as the church is subject unto Christ, so let the wives be to their own husbands in every thing. Husbands, love your wives, even as Christ also loved the church, and gave himself for it; that he might sanctify and cleanse it with the washing of water by the word, that he might present it to himself a glorious church, not having spot, or wrinkle, or any such thing; but that it should be holy and without blemish. So ought men to love their wives as their own bodies. He that loveth his wife loveth himself. For no man ever yet hated his own flesh; but nourisheth and cherisheth it, even as the Lord the church: for we are members of his body, of his flesh, and of his bones. For this cause shall a man leave his father and mother, and shall be joined unto his wife, and they two shall be one flesh. This is a great mystery: but I speak concerning Christ and the church. Nevertheless, let every one of you in particular so love his wife even as himself; and the wife see that she reverence her husband. (Eph. 5:21-33)

The ultimate relationship between man and God is the marriage of Christ and the church. That eternal marriage ought to be mirrored in every Christian marriage. There are profound similarities between human marriage and the relationship of Christ and the church.

The primary biblical passage developing this doctrine is Ephesians, chapter five. The relationship of Christ and the church to the convert is like that of a father (husband) and mother (wife) to their child. Christ (husband) and church (wife) give birth to convert (child). The man in a family is not Christ, but takes the *role* of a Christ-figure in his conduct with his wife and children. The wife is to function toward her husband and children as the church ideally functions. Children fulfill their role by obedience to their parents as though to Christ and the church. Each person benefits his family and himself by fulfilling his role.

The Christian ought to embrace this New Testament concept of marriage and seek to fulfill the living analogy. A change in life pattern from self-centeredness to responsibility for, and fidelity to, another is suggested by this dynamic analogy. Living as a Christian in marriage is living with a sense of duty, love, obedience, sharing, humility, submission and devotion. That which men and women desire to give to God forever, they may in daily miniature give to one another in marriage. An unmarried person may practice similar virtues in human exchanges but under other circumstances than one who is married. If Christian principles rule in a marriage, the relationship between the man and woman will survive a lifetime and God will bless the union.

Physical and spiritual analogies parallel each other. The birth of children is like the spiritual birth of new converts. The Scriptures discuss what it means to be "born again." A new spiritual life is begun in a person through the Lord Jesus Christ. As a child matures, so the Christian matures. Milk is the diet of a child; meat is the diet of a man. A Christian convert is fed on "the milk of the Word" until such time as he can receive "strong meat."

The duty of the husband, if he is to follow Christ's example, may lead him to the point of death for the sake of his wife. She is not to be sacrificed for him, but he for her. Christ died for the church, not the church for Christ. Christ is referred to as going on before to prepare a place for His bride. This self-giving love provides inspiration for the wife to assume her role. The roles of husband and wife should not be clouded by arguments about equality between a man and a woman. The roles differ, but the actors are equal. The child is equal to the father, but he plays a role of obedience to his parents. Yet it is the father's role to sacrifice himself for the child, not the child for the father. The father lays up wealth for the child, and not the child for the father. This fulfills in part the analogy of fatherhood to the conduct of Christ.

Equal Status—Different Roles

Perhaps the concepts of role and equality have been misunderstood. The New Testament teaches that men and women are equal. The apostle Paul asserted that the barriers between Jew and Gentile, between slave and master, between male and female have been broken down (see Gal. 3:28). No longer, argued Paul, is there advantage or disadvantage among persons in the family of God. God never showed respect for one kind of person above the other, but New Testament writers were inspired to strike at prejudices society had developed in confusing role with equality. Jew is not better than Gentile, or vice versa. There is no difference in equality between slave and slave-owner, although mankind required two millennia to apply this equality principle to the victims of slavery. And there ought to be no advantage or disadvantage in being male or female. If a man should argue his superiority over women based on the fact that male (Adam) preceded female (Eve) in the creation, he should be reminded, as the Corinthians were, that the mother precedes her son in procreation (see 1 Cor. 11:11,12).

Some Christian writers overlook these passages in the writings of Paul because they are convinced that he was chauvinistic and believed women to be inferior. These commentators have been reading Paul through biases that come from some traditional interpretations of Paul's meaning. It is not uncommon for widely circulated interpretations to be taken as biblical truth. When his writings are read objectively, it is seen that Paul was not chauvinistic toward women. In harmony with the rest of Scripture, he proclaimed the equality of the sexes.

Equality had been clearly inferred from Genesis 5:2. If the chronology of creation proved anything (and chronology is the common standard used) woman would be superior to man. Adam appeared after the creation of vegetable and animal life. He was the crown of that creation. But woman followed him. Assuming continued upward creative significance the woman would be the acme of God's creative effort.

Relative to male/female status, the Scriptures require only that the order of creation be recognized for the purpose of family organization: God, man (husband), woman (wife), and child. Each was "created" from those who preceded: the male from God, the female from God and the male, and the child from God and the male and the female. The emphasis is on origin and consecutive dependence with lesser responsibility related to descending order. For this reason the husband bears more responsibility than does the wife, and the wife more than the child. It was in Adam, not Eve, that the primary responsibility was lodged. His failure, more than hers, affected the race of man and sinful nature.

Acknowledgment of creation's order is acknowledgment of God's creative gesture.

The attitudes of missionaries in the book of Acts were favorable to women. All churches founded in homes that are identified in the Acts were founded in women's homes. According to the apostle Peter, men and women are joint heirs of heaven, and "joint heirs" means equal. (See 1 Pet. 3:7.) All heirs of heaven are equal. To deny the equality of human beings is to deny a basic biblical principle.

Why then do women appear to be second-class citizens in the church? Partly because of distortions of biblical teachings, partly because most societies created a habit when they sublimated women for thousands of years, and partly because men hoped to protect their wives and children by hiding them from a threatening world and predatory males. Also, anyone knowledgeable about literature and history must be aware that ideas of men have sometimes gained near-biblical authority. John Milton introduced the apple as Eden's forbidden fruit, and since then students have believed an apple tree grew in the center of the Garden. Milton's view of women is sometimes quoted from the Adam and Eve conversation in *Paradise Lost.* Eve spoke to Adam, saying, "God is thy law, thou mine; to know no more is woman's happiest knowledge and her praise." But this is Milton's poetry, not biblical revelation.

The Scriptures define male and female as equal in personhood, but the husband and wife *roles* in marriage differ and may not be perceived as equal. They certainly are different. Perhaps the marriage analogy may be clarified with another metaphor. Suppose a director is preparing to cast a play. He is compelled to make his choice for lead part from two equally superb actors. They are excellent to the degree that critics could not decide which edges out the other in ability. The director must choose. He knows that he is not settling the comparative abilities or rights of the two actors, but merely assigning roles. Even the actors, if they are mature, are aware that the choice does not disparage one or the other. A fine leading actor may relish a cameo role. It is a maxim among drama people that "there are no small parts, only small actors."

The director may finally determine his choice of actors with the flip of a coin. One actor is assigned the lead and the other a strong supporting part. In different circumstances the roles might be reversed. But the decision is made for this occasion. The director will stay with it. If the husband role, the wife role, and the child role are played well, the family drama will become a living Christian witness. The Christian family is perhaps the most effective witness that can ever be given to a world which looks for proofs of God in human experience.

Larry Christensen discussed the marriage analogy in this way:

> Consider the relationship between the Father and the Son. The Son is subject to the Father, yet is equal with the Father. In purely human relationships, subjection often carries with it the stigma of inferiority.

> Not so in a Christian marriage. It is formed on a better model. Husband and wife are one, as the Father and Son are one. The wife is fully equal to the husband, as Christ is equal to God; yet she remains submissive to her husband in all things, as the Son is submissive in all things to the Father. Equality and submis-

sion, far from being opposed to one another, are actually two sides of the same coin. In the Lord, it is neither a degradation of one, nor an exaltation of the other, but answers to the nature of both. In a Christian marriage, you cannot have one without the other. If a wife loses her submission to her husband, she loses her unity with him. If a husband abdicates his responsibility as head, he strikes at the very core of the relationship which God has established between him and his wife.

The Father exalts the Son. He delights to lift Him up, to honor Him. This is the way headship behaves when it is grounded in love. The courtesy which a husband shows toward his wife, the way he honors her before the children, his open and evident esteem for her, is the foundation upon which the wife's respect and trust in her husband is built. And then she, in turn, will acknowledge and exalt her husband, gladly submitting to his authority.[1]

How to Recognize the Marriage Analogy

One's whole life becomes part of the analogy in this New Testament style of marriage. That is to say, virtually every marriage experience may be related to the ideal relationship of Christ with His church. The family becomes a demonstration of what ought to happen in the larger community among Christians, the church as the Body of Christ. Dietrich Bonhoeffer wrote in *Life Together*: "This is the proper metaphor for the Christian community. We are members of a body, not only when we choose to be, but in our whole existence. Every member serves the whole body, either to its health or to its destruction. This is no mere theory; it is a spiritual reality." This existence as a body member with others is readily observable in a marriage. My wife can and does make decisions for the body of her family. Because she makes commitments in my absence, I am careful to fulfill them, careful beyond my obligation to my own promises. This may be an explanation of the fact that "binding on earth" leads to "binding in heaven," as Jesus told His disciples. Their commitment on earth committed Him in heaven.

Human life itself may be seen as an analogy. Individual lives may have larger-than-life meaning. An editor reported: "John Keats once wrote (in his letters) that a man's life, if it be of any worth, must somehow be a continuing allegory." Notice the allegory in the life of Dr. Faust, who sold his soul to Mephistopheles. Analogy is the genius of that story, as it is in *Crime and Punishment*, by Dostoevsky, *A Rose for Emily*, by Faulkner, and other stories.

Analogy was the basis for Jesus' parables. When verbalized, parable and analogy are the same thing. Christian marriages should be living parables of the church and Christ. How Jesus lived may be as much a resource of preaching as the texts of what He said. His life was an analogy. From it we understand His meanings in His words. Why should my life, if Christian, not be an analogy? And my marriage should be a major element of that analogy.

The role distinctions within the family do not fully apply outside of the family, to other men and women. A wife fulfills her role with her husband. She is not called upon to be "submissive" to other men, except in the sense that in the Christian community there are times when any person, man or woman, should submit to leadership for the good of the body. Men and women ought to submit to one another in applicable circumstances (Eph. 5:21). Women do not always submit and men do not escape responsibility to be submissive. Wives submit to their husbands in that special relationship they have with their husbands in the family (Eph. 5:22). The illusion one gains from some New Testament translations and from attitudes in the church is that all Christian women are to be submissive toward all Christian men. This is not the teaching of Scripture. Mary submitted to Joseph, not to other men. Priscilla submitted to Aquila, not to other men. This common pattern of family order seemed useful to the church, but it is the role assignment that applies to marriage. There is opportunity for women in the Christian community. If this is not true, there would have been no place for the evangelist daughters of Philip (see Acts 21:8,9), or the ministries of other women known in the early church (see Rom. 16:1,6; Phil. 4:3).

The Christian marriage analogy of Ephesians 5 is supported by other New Testament passages. But the analogy of marriage was first developed in the Old Testament in the relationship between Israel and God. It was described more fully by various prophets after the children of Israel betrayed their covenant with God and dissolved the relationship. In Jeremiah 3:8 the prophet declared that the marriage has been broken and a bill of divorce had been issued.

In the New Testament the focus turns from real failure to ideal aspiration. There is a shift from human imperfection in the Old Testament to the ideals of ultimate perfection and eternal significance in the New.

The Song of Solomon, a sublime poem, is a detailed analogy of marriage and love, signifying the relationship of God to the imperfect persons who love Him. The entire book is constructed on the analogy of marriage.

The marriage is uneven. At first it was a perfect and dreamlike union, but the bride becomes weak and wanders. The groom is neither unfaithful nor weak. He seeks His bride and accepts her return. She is restored. The bride is man (male and female) and the groom is God.

Refinement of the marriage analogy is to be found in the New Testament, and most clearly in the book of Ephesians. The principle expands like an umbrella over the whole of the New Testament. Jesus on the Mount, Paul before the churches, and John on Patmos sound similar chords in comparing human marriages to the ultimate marriage of Christ to His church.

A reason for the commandment against adultery is that adultery denies the analogy of fidelity to Jesus. Men and women are to have no other god than He. As the pure church worships no other than Christ, so a wife takes no other lover than her husband. And as Christ identifies with no other bride than His church, so a man should be intimate with no other woman than his wife. If either husband or wife were to take another, they would mar the analogy of their marriage. The complete Christian analogy is broken in that particular marriage.

Growth in a marriage is similar to progression in the Christian experience. A couple begins marriage with a love fire of desire. This develops, or ought to, through stages to mature love. The initial zeal and intense love of the Christian convert are like those found in a young lover. (Shakespeare portrays the young lover as "sighing like a furnace.") The more mature Christian's commitment to depth, growth and dedication is like that found in seasoned marriages. As marriage shifts from intense romance and narrow focus at the outset, to depth experience and soul intimacy, so the Christian life advances from the early flame of religious passion to the mature life of faith and service.

Christian Marriage Works—If You Do

Other philosophies of marriage or other solutions to marital difficulties than the Christian marriage analogy seem inadequate by comparison. What better view may be advanced? Yet few Christians seem to be aware of the concept of the marriage analogy, of the application of Ephesians 5. Perhaps the church has failed to teach the meaning of marriage. And the church appears to suffer as a consequence of this failure. Without dynamic Christian families the institutional church falters.

Lack of understanding of the marriage analogy often causes Christians to fail in marriage. After a public talk I received a cursive note from a troubled woman complaining about her total frustration. We met and began counseling sessions. She had an inadequate sense of the meaning of Christian experience, although she was a Christian. She had never tried marriage with the biblical analogy in mind. At the time of her wedding she had been given no meaningful philosophy of marriage. She could not get her marriage on track. She was double-minded, mixing Christian notions with pagan practices. That first marriage was followed by another. One of her two children was fathered by a man married to someone else.

Her distresses seemed to her to be the fault of some unseen and diabolical force. Yet the problem was related to her inability to relate her marriage to a total philosophy of life. She attempted to identify her life with Christianity, but she didn't fully understand the principles. During her last counseling session she confessed that she was under the spell of a new "love" and justified it on the grounds that she had been treated shabbily by the men with whom she had previously shared her life. The pattern of her previous experiences was about to renew itself.

This woman's experiences are like those of many others. They claim to be Christian and presume they are building Christian families, but they do not understand Christian marriage. They are only vaguely conscious of the significance of biblical roles. A Christian youth ought to be taught that his or her life is to be lived as an allegory of God's redemptive purpose. He ought to be shown that God's purpose can be clearly demonstrated as he enters a biblical marriage relationship. Christian marriage is possible for those who choose it, and are willing to work for it. The Scriptures describe the analogy and suggest the resources for achieving its ideal.

Note

1. Larry Christensen, "Which Way the Family?" *Action* (Winter, 1972), p. 23.

CHAPTER THREE

A COMPLETE WORKSHOP

Key points in this chapter include:
- when the family is a workshop for the practice of Christian virtues
- how the family may help one another grow spiritually
- how each family member is identified by a basic virtue
- what relates Christian marriage to other marriage forms
- how Christian marriages develop survival techniques

This is a true saying, If a man desire the office of a bishop, he desireth a good work. A bishop then must be blameless, the husband of one wife, vigilant, sober, of good behavior, given to hospitality, apt to teach; not given to wine, no striker, not greedy of filthy lucre; but patient, not a brawler, not covetous; one that ruleth well his own house, having his children in subjection with all gravity; (for if a man know not how to rule his own house, how shall he take care of the church of God?)

Likewise must the deacons be grave, not double-tongued, not given to much wine, not greedy of filthy lucre; holding the mystery of the faith in a pure conscience. And let these also first be proved; then let them use the office of a deacon, being found blameless. Even so must their wives be grave, not slanderers, sober, faithful in all things. Let the deacons be the husbands of one wife, ruling their children and their own houses well. (1 Tim. 3:1-5,8-12)

Effectiveness in the community of Christians (the church) is partly related to effectiveness in the family (parents and children). Paul the apostle contended that the church leader should be chosen partly because of his effectiveness in family leadership. He was to be married to one wife and to maintain a satisfactory relationship with his children. Christian conduct in his family was a criterion for the election of a deacon, elder or pastor. It was assumed that a man who did not understand how to bring peace to his family may not bring peace to the family of God. Or to put the matter another way, a leader might be discovered because guidance of his family commended him as a leader. His effectiveness in the smaller role recommended him for the larger.

Some theologians believe that offspring of Christian parents possess special potential for favorable response toward God. Covenant theologians substitute baptism for circumcision, making a parallel between the Old and New Testaments in family grace. Both signs are presumed to identify God's promise for the children of parents who are persons of faith. Infant baptism, for them, is public acknowledgement of the grace of God operating in the Christian family. In a similar desire to demonstrate the grace of a Christian family, many fellowships choose to dedicate infants without using baptismal rites. The point made by either ceremony is that Christian marriage exerts a salutary effect upon children born of that marriage.

There is, then, a reservoir of God's grace that may and ought to be tapped for the benefit of family members. Most benefits relate to spiritual life which cause improvement in individuals; from these individuals improvement takes place in the marriage. Marriage quality is the summary of the persons in it. For that reason some persons, in their spiritual growth, compel marriage growth. Other members, through their rebellion, selfishness or the like, introduce tension, pain and unhappiness into marriage. This is one reason why marriages are uneven. A mate, or child, or both mates and several children reject their personal responsibility to become the persons they were meant to be. One member may build the marriage while the other undermines it. Virtue or fault is in persons, not in the marriage.

Marriage, then, is a workshop where evil or good attitudes and acts may be practiced. In a Christian marriage each person should choose virtuous paths and devote conscious effort to promoting and following them. They assure success. There are eternal resources available to those who wish to make their marriages Christian.

Marriage Is for Better, Not for Worse

Man and wife should expect to learn virtues from one another in marriage. My own experience is a case in point. If my mother were asked to describe what I was like before marriage, she would present a very different picture from the way my wife would describe me now. I have overheard their exchanges from time to time, as they compared notes on the "old" me and the "now" me.

As a young man I was impatient, but I learned to practice patience in my relationships with my own family members. On one occasion, in a fury I drove away from my sisters because they were not ready at 3:00 P.M., the time we agreed upon. I was the only driver in the family and had nothing better to do than pilot them to their appointment. And they were walking out of the house when I drove away. They were all of two minutes late.

Early in my marriage impatience often surfaced. At times my conduct created a tense atmosphere so that by the time my wife and children were ready to go, we gained no pleasure in our project.

Currently, I may stand at the front door, shift from foot to foot, and sigh heavily, but at least I do not carry on a tirade about the immorality of lateness or the virtues of doing things as I do them. And I would not drive away as I did from my sisters. My marriage has taught me patience, and I sense that in return my family has become more patient with me. The lessons have benefited me. I receive in accord with what I give.

Virtues can be discovered, developed, controlled, strengthened. When they are they become strong, whereas the exponent—the person—becomes meek. Virtues become tough, whereas the exponent becomes tender. They become makers of change, causing the exponent to become a better self. Patience may be used as a case in point.

"Patience is a virtue," declares an old but true cliché. Patience is not resignation or shyness or weakness. It is active, strong and creative. Patience may instruct me to wait for a better time to do what I otherwise wish to do on the spur of the moment.

I may have to summon patience out of my will. When I am forced to wait for my family to get ready to go out, I may have to seek some temporary activity to reduce my tension, like reading several pages from a book, or making a short phone call, or assisting in a chore that is causing delay.

"Why are we late so often?" I began analyzing the problem by asking questions of myself. "Am I at peace with myself? What do I need to do to be tranquil and serene?" Then I questioned my wife and children, "How long are you going to take?" They perceived that line of questioning as judgmental. I tried again, "What may I do to help with the children?" Other devices followed. I suggested the time for us to begin to get ready rather than the hour for leaving the house. And I "fudged" on the exit time, setting it a quarter hour earlier than required.

Soon my frustration declined. My voice was better modulated. I did not make quick, and sometimes panicky, trips from room to room. I appeared less discouraged to my family. As my wife and I calmly worked together we discovered a number of ways to assure getting away on time. She even changed her hairstyle to something simple but attractive in order to meet our schedule expectations.

Perhaps the best technique we discovered was that we could act out that which we wished to feel. We would act patient and thereby become patient. We knew how we ought to function so we made ourselves do what we ought. Because love and loving acts meant more to us than rigid schedules and expectations, we discovered a creative patience that led us into real patience. We learned that we could control our emotions rather than be controlled by them. What better place than marriage to practice this great virtue—marriage with its repetitions, trial and error, love and acceptance?

Another old tendency was to spend much of my energy on my own interest, which is selfish. As time passed, the exigencies of family life changed me. I learned how to put my wife and children before myself in my plans. Some persons never make the self-other transition after marriage. In counseling I notice that many persons feel driven to divorce when they continue to center on themselves. It is possible that selfishness is the leading cause of marital failure.

Perhaps the greatest error in some of the women's liberation groups is that they attack men and male-dominated institutions for selfishness, but they seek to replace it with a selfishness of their own. Liberation literature sometimes affirms virtue in a self-centeredness that goes beyond appropriate self-esteem. Some champions of rights find little place for sacrificial treatment for children, and family duty is denigrated. Christians ought to be concerned with human rights and equity for women, but not at the expense of family duty. Men should support equal rights for women because of justice, putting aside their own selfishness.

By living with another person in the close relationship of marriage I learned to restrain my desire to have my own way. It was a learning process and required effort. I discovered that gentleness and self-control, biblical virtues, could be learned and practiced in marriage even by an aggressive person. If I could not practice these virtues in marriage, what was the significance of my Christian life?

A good place to begin the strategy of acting out—practicing in the family—all the personal virtues is to take seriously the list Paul calls the "fruit of the Spirit" (see Gal. 5:22): love, joy, peace, longsuffering, gentleness, goodness, faith, meekness and temperance. These virtues can be effectively practiced until they become life and marriage habits.

Included in marriage are three special virtues that call family members to duty. Each virtue relates to all members, but each is assigned its particular champion. The husband is commissioned to love, the wife is called to submit, and the child is commanded to obey.

A husband who loves his wife grants all her rights, eagerly meets her needs, gently cares for her interests, always protects her, adjusts his conduct assuming that she is the "weaker vessel." (She may not be weaker, but he *assumes* that she is.) All his actions are to be motivated by love. He practices love throughout his marriage.

A wife is the champion of submission—submission in the biblical sense. To be submissive does not indicate that the wife is inferior in herself or that she has an inferior position in the family hierarchy. Submission does not deny equality and partnership.[1] Submission is wholly voluntary. If a wife does not voluntarily submit, she cannot be commanded to submit for to command submission is a contradiction in terms. If commands are given and response follows, that response is not submission but obedience, and obedience does not belong to husband and wife but to their children.

The great example of submission, as we discussed in an earlier chapter, was Jesus Christ who voluntarily submitted to His Father, to His disciples, and ultimately to His enemies. Certainly, He was also loving and obedient. Each family member finds his exemplar in Jesus Christ.

Obedience is the child's primary virtue. As Jesus subjected Himself to Mary and Joseph, children are to subject themselves to their parents. Obedience learned in childhood mirrors itself decades later in the self-discipline of husband or wife. Begun in youth, discipline is honed in marriage and provides motivation for life and godliness.

Marriage Requires the Best, Not the Leftovers

At some point in my marriage—I have forgotten the moment—I determined not to treat anyone better than I treated my wife. I had seen men treat women very solicitously—holding a door, engaging in gracious conversation, assisting with a chair, offering gifts, or doing onerous chores. They appeared to treat women as special persons. Each was the gracious host. Then I saw them with their wives. Any treatment would do. They would get in the car and start it. If the poor women did not move rapidly to get into the passenger side, they might find themselves sprawled on the curb.

One woman reported in counseling that she had learned to rush to the car before her husband started the motor. If she did not, he would creep the automobile along the drive while she was trying to get in. She seriously requested that I order him to "hold the car until I get in." He acknowledged the habit and said jokingly he liked to see her run. I encouraged him to find other sport. A different man told me solemnly that he did the same thing. On one occasion he braked suddenly and his wife hit the car, sprawling over the fender and hood. She was pregnant.

The principle that the family is the workshop for the practice of Christian virtues applies to all members of the family. Each parent ought to teach, by precept and conduct, an unselfish style of life. I wish to be a gentleman at all times. But if I cannot show consideration for my wife, I will not do so for other persons. I have learned that being a gentleman with her ultimately causes me to function better toward others. In fact, I found that nearly every relationship improved when my life with my family improved. The principle is broadly applicable: Children who are surly to their parents will likely be surly with others. It is something of a truism that the way in which a young man treats his mother provides important clues to the way he will treat his wife. A daughter's conduct toward her father is a clue to the treatment a husband will receive.

There are elements of Christian family life that shall also be found in heaven. One of these is continuing fellowship with the same group of people. If I cannot, day by day, be loving toward these people on earth, why should I believe that I am ready for life immortal shared with an unchanging population? What I can or cannot do for 50 years on earth may have something to do with my functioning in the eternal state.

Other Forms of Marriage

In this book the accent is on happy and successful Christian marriage. Even if they are otherwise devout, couples may reject the Christian view of marriage if they wish, but if they do they will not enjoy the ideal marriage defined in the New Testament. They will not provide, in their marriages, the witness of Christ and the church.

Couples may, in some other form of marriage, be happy and live in socially acceptable ways. There is no attempt here to diminish other forms of marriage relationships, some of which appear more effective than that of many couples who affirm Christianity but do not practice it. The superiority of Christian marriage does not rest upon the success or failure of other forms.

A civil marriage with a special and personal contract may work well for a couple. Although seldom used in English-speaking countries, special or family contract marriages have been well known for centuries and are standard in some countries where divorce is uncommon. They serve their societies well; and who can say that personal unhappiness in those marriages is any greater than that found in the English-speaking world? The assumption among romantics, that contracted marriages are unhappy, is fallacious.

Cultural marriage forms are sometimes developed to meet special needs in the tribe, society or nation. Ancient Israel developed Levirate marriage in order to protect widows and assure the ongoing of an heirship for the deceased husband's family. The story of Ruth is a narrative of a Levirate marriage. Ruth's husband, Mahlon, died. Ruth returned with Naomi, her mother-in-law, to his homeland, where she sought to marry Mahlon's next of kin. He opted in favor of Boaz, next to him in the blood line. Ruth and Boaz were married, and their first child, Obed, was delivered into the arms of Naomi to be identified as the heir of Mahlon. Levirate marriage was an accommodation from God to assist in social control and to provide security for women in Israel.

Apparently Jesus noted the possibility of "common-law" marriage when He declared that the act of sexual intimacy between a man and a harlot constituted marriage. Even though the persons in such a liaison would not likely continue faithful to each other, the "marriage" might become acceptable if they did, and if they carried appropriate responsibilities.

We support effective and honorable marriages however they are established. Even less-than-ideal marriages can be made to work. Non-Christians converting to Christ should not make their new faith an excuse for dissolving their less-than-perfect marriages. New resources in Christ may rescue failing relationships.

Needed: Survival Techniques for Marriage

Persons need each other. Some human needs are intense and demanding. We live on the verge of exploiting others to gain what we desire. Family members especially may unethically use each other. To avoid the evil, Christian virtues like those referred to in this chapter need to be understood and practiced. Even so, marriage is a balance between using and being used. Those who misunderstand that balance, seeing only one side of the issue, may denigrate marriage. They resist sacrifice and downgrade or dismiss benefits that accrue to a marriage partner.

Critics may attack marriage, not so much with facts as opinions. Some arguments are non sequiturs; they do not follow logically. For example, according to *Time* magazine, British biologist Alexander Comfort asserted: "A husband or wife is expected to be mother, father, child, uncles and aunts; this is a greater burden than any one human being can possibly carry." And what is his answer to these role problems? According to *Time*: "Group sex is a way of sharing the burden, and Comfort anticipates a future 'in which settled couples engage openly in a side range of sexual relations with friends.' "[2]

What do sexual relationships with friends have to do with making mothers, fathers, aunts and uncles to meet role needs in the family? Presumed to be a scholar, Comfort does not, according to *Time*, argue persuasively on several issues. The magazine is kind to Comfort, not pointing out some of his serious errors, such as: "Most people have been married more than once, and adultery is universally tolerated. Open marriage would simply legitimise what we already live."[3] It is unbelievable that a sophisticated person would make statements like these when he knew, at the time of his statement, that two-thirds to three-fourths of marrieds live with their original spouse. And adultery is still frowned upon, even though there may be no legal sanctions against it. Comfort, like others who would diminish traditional marriage and fidelity, makes cavalier statements about life based on bizarre or minority conduct—conduct unduly accented by the media. They make war on the American family. And they presume that their attacks have won the war.

It is vital that survival techniques be developed and practiced in families. Enemies emerge, sometimes unsuspected, from any direction. Among the enemies are the "Dreaded D's"—debt, divorce, disease and death. How money is managed, how tensions are confronted, how health is maintained, and how death is met are matters which fall hard on human beings. Families, by creative and cooperative approaches, ease the weights of life's burdens for their members. By learning, in the close relationships compelled by family life, to care for one another is to lift devastating burdens from each as situations arise. The one under pressure may, on another occasion, become the comforting and sharing member to the person who assisted him.

There is in creative Christian marriage a quality of awe and morality. This grows out of spiritual perceptions. Life in humanity is awesome. When it is guided by the morality of God as revealed in the Scriptures, there follows a family beauty that borders on devotion. And when husband and wife, with child, recognize that truth, rising to it, they know there are possibilities that are seldom even hinted at in the literature of marriage. It may have been this insight that caused Martin Luther to say, "Marriage compels us to believe."

During January 1975, our elder daughter, Sharon, was married. After the ceremony, special guests were invited to share a wedding dinner. My wife, Sharon's mother, refused all assistance in preparing the meal. She wished to do the work herself for her daughter. Awaiting the call to eat, the guests offered best wishes to Sharon and Gordon, the groom. One by one, each made remarks in the hearing of all. At last a turn came for Jody, our younger daughter. Seated next to me, Jody stood up, looked at her sister and began to weep. I thought she would sit down because of embarrassment, but she insisted on making her remarks. And I was deeply moved.

Jody said, "Sharon, I wish for you the most wonderful thing I can think of—that your marriage will be like mom's and dad's. It is the most creative and beautiful thing I have ever seen."

I was lifted with a sense of gratitude. My only disappointment was that Jody's and Sharon's mother was not in the room to hear what our youngest child had to say. Why should we be so blessed at a time in history when children were denigrating their parents? Why did I hear what I would most wish to hear if my best wishes were granted? The answer is in creative Christian marriage, with all its privileges and responsibilities. They emanate from the theory of biblical marriage and are made possible by the authority of the Holy Spirit. By that Spirit came growth and acceptance. And that recognition of vital assistance made us humble in the words of our daughter.

It was growth in spiritual truth and love that helped my wife and me cultivate our marriage. And love learned from God sustained it. My own experience in developing love for my wife is personally dramatic for me.

My love grew, and the first love now appears shallow by comparison with that which I now experience. This observation does not degrade the first love. Without it there would have been no succeeding stages. By reviewing my marriage, I am able to follow the changes in my life, character, and understanding through the years. My life developed a new logic. I believed that God loved my wife and she loved Him. I believed that I loved God and He loved me. There had to be something wrong with one or both of us if we could not love each other. That logic became compelling.

Notes

1. Paul K. Jewett, *Man as Male and Female* (Grand Rapids: Wm. B. Eerdmans Publishing Co., 1975), pp. 130,131.
2. Alexander Comfort, "Swinging Future," *Time* magazine, January 8, 1973, p. 35.
3. Ibid.

PART TWO

RELIGION

For God wants his children to live in peace and harmony.
(1 Cor. 7:15, *TLB*)

CHAPTER FOUR

FAITH THAT FIGHTS MARRIAGE

Key points in this chapter include:
- what are common religious differences in marriages
- how religious differences affected several eminent Bible marriages
- how to sustain one's faith in severe family circumstances

And it came to pass by the way in the inn, that the Lord met him, and sought to kill him. Then Zipporah took a sharp stone, and cut off the foreskin of her son, and cast it at his feet, and said, Surely a bloody husband art thou to me. So he let him go: then she said, A bloody husband thou art, because of the circumcision.

Then Satan answered the Lord, and said, Doth Job fear God for nought? Hast not thou made a hedge about him, and about his house, and about all that he hath on every side? thou hast blessed the work of his hands, and his substance is increased in the land.

And Abigail came to Nabal; and, behold, he held a feast in his house, like the feast of a king; and Nabal's heart was merry within him, for he was very drunken: wherefore she told him nothing, less or more, until the morning light. But it came to pass in the morning, when the wine was gone out of Nabal, and his wife had told him these things, that his heart died within him, and he became as a stone. And it came to pass about ten days after, that the Lord smote Nabal, that he died. (Exod. 4:24-26; Job 1:9,10; 1 Sam. 25:36-38)

Religion is a strong adhesive in an effective marriage. It is commonly recognized that Christian faith has contributed to making better marriages than has any single secular influence. When decline in marriage solidarity occurs in the general society, decline in religion is usually blamed. The Durants, in *The Lessons of History*, refer repeatedly to the negative effects of religious and moral decline on virtually all social institutions. Other authors strike the same chord.

Divided Faith Marriages—A Growing Phenomenon

In analyzing the influence of Christianity on history, writers tend to focus on Roman Catholicism and main-line liberal Protestantism. They assume smaller conservative groups hold strong control over their adherents. These smaller groups are assumed to have better marriage records but the samples are not large enough to affect society significantly. It is likely that newer information would show some withering of marriage solidarity among couples related to evangelical churches. The secular society has made deep inroads into Christian culture, and church leaders are sensing loss in the quality of life among church members, even when there is growth in membership rolls. In order to accommodate cultural shifts, a number of conservative denominations have liberalized policies concerning sexual practices, divorce and remarriage. Some ministers in evangelical churches have quietly divorced and remarried. Many others have recently been willing to officiate in a marriage of divorced persons.

Nevertheless, the record of marriage solidarity is firmer in the evangelical or conservative church than in other institutions. More dependable statistical evidence on marriage is needed. Improved scholarship is being applied to the study of evangelical families. Not all research relating to church life and activity survives scrutiny. Results of studies published by certain secular as well as religious sources are questionable. The lack of scholarship (inadequate samples, few controls, and the like) in several secular projects suggests that their preju-

53

dices are showing. In similar ways, prejudices or unwarranted sympathies have been demonstrated by some evangelicals in making assertions about their own interests. Scholars on one side of an issue cannot make excuses for shoddy work by comparing it to other unsatisfactory efforts. Quality needs to be raised all along the line in order to produce data that are trustworthy.

Anyone closely associated with Christian and secular organizations will observe greater solidarity of marriage in Christian communities. Families in these communities are generally happier and more committed to moral values arising from both biblical and cultural traditions. Studies of longtime evangelical families show that the integrity of marriage is rather well maintained.

Nevertheless, religious faith does lead in many instances to considerable unhappiness between husband and wife, and especially between parents and children. This unhappiness may be found in families which are avowedly Christian as well as those partly divided by differential elements of vital faith.

Problems Come in Different Packages

Common religious differences in a family include: (a) Christian and non-Christian members who force conflicting viewpoints on each other, (b) denominational identities that divide loyalties, (c) doctrinal beliefs that are presumed by one person to be vital, and (d) factional disputes that drive wedges between family members. A short summary of these issues will achieve the purpose here.

Faith Differences. Differences in faith between husband and wife provide a major cause of marital conflict. These differences may be deliberately intensified by either mate as excuses to evade duties. Rationalization is often used by Christian women who do not wish to continue their relationships with their husbands. A wife may use the argument that she has become a Christian and consequently does not wish to maintain friendship with the world. The most obvious worldly relationship is intimacy with her non-Christian husband. She may have wished to shed her husband all along. She finds the religious argument "What fellowship hath God with Belial?" to be effective in winning support from some of her close friends. There is no doubt about who is on God's side and who is on Belial's. Other reasons for her disappointment may be valid, but they are lost in the sacred shroud drawn over events. Honesty would have been the better policy and may have led to a solution. Evangelization of a non-Christian husband is hindered when he sees his wife using distortions of religion to achieve opposite goals (rejection) than those (acceptance) which Christ means to achieve.

Differences may be profound, causing marital breakup between persons who are "unequally yoked together." Non-Christian mates, especially husbands, may force issues because of their animosities toward the religion of their wives. Crude language, insistence upon untypical behavior, or harassment relative to the exercise of spiritual duties may become forms of cruelty and intimidation. If peaceful coexistence in a mixed marriage is no longer possible, and the non-Christian mate wishes to be free, that person should be released. The teaching of the Scripture is that God has called the Christian to peace, but if peace is not possible, after the child of faith has made every effort to gain it, then the reality of breakup is to be accepted. This situation is described in 1 Corinthians 7:12-16:

> If a Christian has a wife who is not a Christian,
> but she wants to stay with him anyway, he

must not leave her or divorce her. And if a Christian woman has a husband who isn't a Christian, and he wants her to stay with him, she must not leave him. For perhaps the husband who isn't a Christian may become a Christian with the help of his Christian wife. And the wife who isn't a Christian may become a Christian with the help of her Christian husband. Otherwise, if the family separates, the children might never come to know the Lord; whereas a united family may, in God's plan, result in the children's salvation. But if the husband or wife who isn't a Christian is eager to leave, it is permitted. In such cases the Christian husband or wife should not insist that the other stay, for God wants his children to live in peace and harmony. For, after all, there is no assurance to you wives that your husbands will be converted if they stay; and the same may be said to you husbands concerning your wives *(TLB)*.

The Christian, committed to biblical interests and life-style, may find objectionable the habits and attitudes of his non-Christian mate. Or the non-Christian may object to what he believes to be the narrow and suffocating life-style of the Christian. Conflicts multiply. A believer/unbeliever marriage is twice as vulnerable to divorce as a believer/believer marriage. Even so, a marriage with at least one Christian partner will more likely survive than a marriage in which neither mate has personal faith.

Denominational Differences. There may be pressures created by differences in denominational or other religious loyalties between Christian mates. Some fellowships are provincial to the degree that if a member defects to another Christian group he is ostracized by friends and parents. They may never speak to him again. Or doctrinal differences may divide family members so that they cannot converse civilly with one another, and may reject mutual fellowship. If Luther and Zwingli could not shake hands because of their differences in the communion ritual, it may be expected that average lay persons might be even less willing to accept differences between themselves.

Doctrinal Disputes. One mate may attempt to gain psychological authority over the other by tenaciously advancing a doctrine or practice. The pressure may constitute hypocrisy. There may be insistence by husband or wife that their children should follow a faith that the urging father or mother will not follow. Some fathers have demanded that their children should be reared in a faith to which they themselves no longer adhere. They may insist that their wives oversee the training, even though the wives may have no similar religious tradition and do not agree with it.

Factional Arguments. Some of the hottest religious arguments relate to factional differences over ministers, buildings, programs, or some other non-theological issue in the church. These emotional issues within a church have split families that otherwise appeared to be solid. In some cases divorce has resulted.

Moses and Zipporah Had Their Troubles

Several biblical illustrations suggest the depth of feeling that emerges from religious differences. The experience of conflict between *Moses and his wife, Zipporah,* was dramatic and troublesome. This is a significant case because Moses was a leading character in the history of Judeo-Christian faith. The presumption is that if a major religious leader encountered problems, it is to be expected that persons with fewer spiritual resources for life might have similar problems. The laws and life of Moses are accepted as guides by men and women of faith. They hold a significant place in the Old Testament.

The dramatic incident that sheds greatest light on Moses' marital life is recorded in Exodus 4:24,25. Moses married Zipporah, a woman who had no background in his faith. As a fugitive he had fled to the community in which Zipporah lived. One might speculate on his motivations. Perhaps marriage to one who was not a member of the tribes of Israel would provide some protection for him in his self-imposed exile. During the following years his spiritual life and high purpose revived. He introduced the faith of his fathers to his in-laws, and he himself began to practice greater obedience to Jehovah. Zipporah, however, apparently encountered difficulty accepting this faith.

Ordinarily Moses and Zipporah did not press religious issues to a conclusion. But when the matter of circumcision arose on the way to Egypt, her sensitivities were strained. Although offended, she reluctantly accepted circumcision of her son as a requirement from God. In a tense confrontation with her husband, she performed the surgery on her son. But the rift between her and Moses was not healed. She abandoned him and returned to her father's house, taking her sons with her. It would appear that Moses' marriage had been destroyed for reasons of religion.

Moses and Zipporah were ultimately reconciled, but the return of Zipporah created additional tension. This was dramatically illustrated in the judgment of Miriam, Moses' sister. Her criticism of Zipporah led God to send a plague of leprosy upon Miriam. It is not clear whether Miriam's attitudes were negative because Zipporah was unschooled in the faith of Jehovah, or because Zipporah had abandoned her husband on the way to Egypt, or because Zipporah was of another race. Some authorities believe Moses' wife was negroid and prejudice flourished then as now. It is clear that she was not an Israelite.

Job Had His Problems, Too

Perhaps Job and his family fit the general pattern of a home divided on spiritual matters. It was relatively easy for Job's wife to accept her husband's religious position when all went well. However, her faith seems to have been the fairweather variety withering, somewhat under the heat of trial. Job and his wife probably shared basic views but differed in their degree of commitment. After all else had fallen to tragedy—the collapse of his fortune and the death of his children—Job was faced with a final loss, the empathy of his wife. Her words are not easy to analyze, and Job's wife has suffered from a bad press. She did not tell Job to curse God. The Hebrew word here translated "curse" is everywhere else in the Old Testament translated "bless." She said, "Bless God and die." Job's sufferings and her labors seemed too great for her. Her emotions may have tired, her tolerances worn thin.

The impression given by the Hebrew text is that Job's wife was not as totally unsympathetic as commentators and preachers make her out to be. She appears to have had faith, even if it was weak. But there was serious religious tension between husband and wife. When finally Job was restored in wealth and children, no mention of his wife is made. It is not known if she, or another, became the beneficiary of that restoration.

One of the most dramatic biblical illustrations of religious division between husband and wife is found in the relationship of *Nabal and Abigail* (1 Sam. 25:2-43). Nabal, "churlish and evil in his doings," was married to Abigail, "a woman of good understanding, and of a beautiful countenance." Abigail employed her spiritual sensitivity to protect the life of her husband, although his death would have brought personal relief to her.

Abigail's loyalty to Nabal and the quality of life she manifested did not obscure the depravity of her husband. If anything, her virtue accented it. She ultimately understood what he had become. She left him to God. Her consistency of life did not turn her husband from his ways, nor did his life corrupt hers. She did not use her faith nor his evil as an excuse to relieve herself of an unsatisfactory situation. Her conduct and attitude may serve as a model for those involved in similar marriages today.

Solutions Are Possible in Divided Faith Families

What are some of the solutions available to family members divided in faith? The apostle Paul discussed the issue of peace in 1 Corinthians, chapter seven. He asserted that Christians are to be at peace, and this peace is to be demonstrated in the family. If the split-faith family is to be broken up, the non-Christian member must take the initiative for the break. The Christian partner may not use his Christianity as an excuse for extricating himself from an unsatisfactory or unhappy situation. Nor is he to create circumstances that force his mate to move toward dissolution.

Troubled marriages ought to be counseled early in their development. Even if the situation has been neglected for years, the parties should not give up. It is true that research results show little success where assistance has been delayed. Yet, the solution to Moses' marital problems came late in life. The conflict had been intense. Zipporah returned home after her dramatic clash with Moses. Her father, Jethro, apparently received her back. Jethro delayed his efforts to effect reconciliation until Moses had achieved his major goal, leading Israel out of Egypt and into the wilderness. Then he served as an effective marriage counselor. When the time was expedient, he returned Zipporah and the children to Moses, and through his help and advice the rift was healed. It is likely that in the interim Moses had sifted out some of his personal problems. He may have become more empathic toward his wife. Zipporah must have become convinced that Jehovah was with her husband and that her own reactions were unjustified. The wisdom of Jethro appears to have been shared without harshness or favoritism on his part. The point to be made is that Moses and Zipporah must have admitted their need for counsel and accepted advice. In this instance it came from a close member of the family. Its success was dependent not only on Jethro's wisdom, but on Moses' openness to receive counsel from his father-in-law.

The specifics of Job's family situation are not entirely available to us, for the book focuses on the ordeal of Job as he witnessed and suffered it. Only glimpses of the family are provided. Job loved his family. He presumed ultimate solutions to their difficulties would be spiritual because the problems were spiritual. According to the observation of Satan, Job, having few personal problems, could afford to be religious. Satan's testing of Job's motivation resulted in a series of depressing experiences for Job. Under pressure Job remained devoted to God. His wife, on the other hand, doubted the worth of life under this tension. Job emerged through his tragedy by maintaining faith, assuming responsibility and finding the balance necessary for working his way out of problems.

One of the lessons of sacred biography is that faith can be sustained in the face of the most severe circumstances. Marriage often provides trying circumstances that test personal faith. Effective solutions are found in genuine devotion to God. In addition to those cited above, a number of other Old Testament biographies might be reviewed as examples of how marital difficulties may be solved through faith. The emphasis on differences between the patriarchs, their wives and children occupies more than half of the book of Genesis. Husbands and wives may find significant insights for their marriages through a study of these passages.

I am confident that, if my life situation required it, I would find ways of living with a person who is not a Christian. I would expect to be able to carry through my devotional experience and select a church in which I might grow spiritually without offending my mate.

A person must be careful not to do God's work *for* Him. Some Christian marriage partners use clever little strategies to trap their mates into believing what they wish them to believe. The Christian partner may place religious materials, with special underlinings, in the path of a family member, may preach unsolicited little sermonettes, may put on the countenance of a sulking prophet, and may interpret his own views as final truth. But such devices cloud the true Christian message and seldom lead to desired goals.

One woman of my acquaintance left Bibles and tracts about her house so that her husband would "stumble over" or discover "by chance" her clearly-marked passages and find faith in Christ. A visitor might easily see that this man was determined to resist so overt an effort. How much better it would have been if she had simply lived out the Christian faith as a loving wife. Her life and conduct could provide a spiritual thrust far more forceful than a printed page. The woman's life, lived without judgmentalism, might have motivated her husband to search the Scriptures or subject himself to preaching, and to decision.

Couples should be encouraged to know that many of "God's favorite families," as represented by the appearance of their biographies in the Bible, were deeply troubled by problems similar to our own. And those ancients managed their situations with varying degrees of success as we do. They do show by their experiences that success is possible when persons are willing to utilize spiritual resources, willing to accept one another, to yield on some issues, and to moderate expectations to realistic levels.

CHAPTER FIVE

FAITH THAT FREES MARRIAGE

Key points in this chapter include:
- how we use religious aggression to force others to our choice of life-style
- why family devotions and church attendance divide some families
- what is meant by "liberating Christian faith"

And they brought in the ark of the Lord, and set it in his place, in the midst of the tabernacle that David had pitched for it: and David offered burnt offerings and peace offerings before the Lord. And as soon as David had made an end of offering burnt offerings and peace offerings, he blessed the people in the name of the Lord of hosts. And he dealt among all the people, even among the whole multitude of Israel, as well to the women as men, to every one a cake of bread, and a good piece of flesh, and a flagon of wine. So all the people departed every one to his house. Then David returned to bless his household. And Michal the daughter of Saul came out to meet David, and said, How glorious was the king of Israel today, who uncovered himself today in the eyes of the handmaids of his servants, as one of the vain fellows shamelessly uncovereth himself! And David said unto Michal, It was before the Lord, which chose me before thy father, and before all his house, to appoint me ruler over the people of the Lord, over Israel: therefore will I play before the Lord. And I will yet be more vile than thus, and will be base in mine own sight: and of the maidservants which thou hast spoken of, of them shall I be had in honor. Therefore Michal the daughter of Saul had no child unto the day of her death. (2 Sam. 6:17-23)

Religion may be used as a means of control, not so much to apply God's will in a family, but to enforce the will of a parent, mate or child. Religious aggression, as the phrase is used here, does not represent genuine Christian zeal or understanding, but bigotry and self-serving assertiveness. A father may claim Christian authority as head of his house to gain what he desires for his own benefit. Perhaps most persons have observed or experienced the tension and disharmony that develop when a man demands, in statement or attitude, that his wife and children submit to his will. He does not return love and compassion, gentleness and generosity, strength and example in exchange for their deference to his leadership. His approach arises from a misunderstanding of the biblical principles of leadership and submission.

Religious Aggression in Personal Life-Style

Sometimes a parent forces a personal life-style on his family as a principle of Christian belief, when it is really a matter of culture and tradition. During the period following the rise of the Beatles musical group and the student confrontations that began in late 1964, a significant change in grooming and life-style took place among young men and women.

Hair length became a symbolic issue. The length of hair worn by many male students broke from styles preferred by the majority of parents and older adults. Tensions between generations became severe, yet, no one could prove that one style was preferred by God over some other style. A number of biblical passages were quoted and sometimes distorted to provide each side an aura of religious authority. Youths identified with some features in the life-style of Jesus or John the Baptist; elders quoted the apostle Paul, who advised the Corinthians that long hair for males was against nature.

The Old Testament was also invoked in the controversy. Samson, Absalom and Samuel were called upon as witnesses. Absalom permitted his hair to grow and apparently was vain about his appearance. Fleeing from his father's general, he lost his life when his hair became entangled in a tree. Samson and Samuel (and later John the Baptist) appear to have taken Nazarite vows which forbade cutting one's hair. Because of special dedication to God, these men neither cut their hair nor drank strong drink.

Larger issues may create religious tensions in a family. The text opening this chapter provides a case in point. David's wife, Michal, was reared in a king's palace. Her husband had lived in the fields and cared for sheep. The differences in their life-styles were dramatic.

On one occasion David returned from a successful campaign and celebrated his delight by leaping and dancing in the street before his happy subjects. He praised God for success and distributed gifts to his people. At length he returned to his house to celebrate with his family. But Michal was embarrassed by David's street conduct. Apparently she had observed her husband's behavior before the people. From her balcony she had been shielded from the peasants. Their easy, casual, rough ways offended her. She preferred the stately worship of the tabernacle, the robed priests, the fine choirs. Seeing her husband openly express his feelings in so raucous a fashion offended her sensitivities. She sarcastically berated him. The argument that followed was severe and ended the intimate relationship between them. Although they remained married, David never again approached Michal's chamber. She was childless, which, according to the ancient culture, was a dishonor to her.

Religion was often a matter of tension for venerable Abraham and his wife. Sarah was at odds with Abraham over the promise of an heir. She laughed at her husband for his faith that God would give them a child. Sarah had well passed the normal period of childbearing for women. In time she concocted a way to overcome Abraham's fanaticism. She arranged for Hagar, her slave girl, to substitute for her, and Hagar bore Ishmael. But later, tension arose between Sarah and Abraham over the matter. The events surrounding this lapse of faith in God's promise resulted in a sordid story.

Like other couples who basically accept the same faith, Sarah and Abraham went through periods of disagreement so extreme that it might occasionally seem that they did not believe in the same God. In the end it became obvious to Sarah that her husband did have genuine insight into God's will. She accented her humble admission by naming their son *Isaac*, which is translated "laughter." She had laughed at her husband and at God's promise, and for the rest of her life she would be reminded of her lapse of faith when she spoke the name of her son.

Both couples—Michal and David, and Sarah and Abraham—experienced religious aggression within their marriages. Michal ought to have learned to tolerate David's style, not necessarily for herself but at least for him. He was programmed to experience life differently from his wife. The type of communication he found comfortable and meaningful was unsophisticated, open, energetic, casual and audible. Michal preferred a liturgy, a worshipful atmosphere, a sense of propriety and an intensely private expression of faith. He was loud and boisterous; she was sophisticated and muted in her expression.

Michal appears to have lost in the exchange, not because of her lack of faith but because of her disregard for the genuineness of her husband's worship. Who is to say which pattern, David's or Michal's, is superior? Since

God is the only one who understands human motivations: husbands and wives need to leave judgment of their mates in such matters to Him.

There is a remarkable variety of ways in which Christian faith and devotion can be expressed. This has been my observation as a speaker in different fellowships and denominations. I cannot, in honesty, say one is better than another, even though I am personally more comfortable in the practice of a particular style. When I speak to a group I respect their practices. However, habits of a given group change as well. Asked to speak at a conference of a large formal denomination, I selected a wardrobe for myself in keeping with what I thought was the tradition of the people to whom I would speak. To my astonishment, I was the only one present at the first meeting who wore a suit, white shirt and tie. The men looked like recent returnees from Hawaii in their flowered aloha shirts.

For another conference two weeks later I selected casual wear. The sponsoring denomination was known as informal in attitudes and unstructured in their worship services. The conference was held at a mountain retreat. But I was the only man on the platform wearing sports shirt and slacks. All the others who took part and most of the men in the audience wore suits, shirts and ties.

I was further surprised to find that the first group, the more formal, sang with enthusiasm and occasionally clapped their hands or raised them above their heads. This seemed incongruous to me, based on my earlier acquaintance with the denomination. But I was just as surprised by the second group for they sang without overt physical expression. The two fellowships appeared to have exchanged their ways of doing things. In spite of my surprise, I found no personal problem in accepting both styles and recognizing the sincerity and usefulness of each. I maintained my own style of expression without self-consciousness or judgmentalism. The adaptations I had to make for these two conferences were in areas that did not violate my values.

How Should a Family Handle Religious Tension?

Within a family, differences in religious practice may cause distortion of the meaning of Christian conviction and love. A number of common problems divide family members. The two most frequent seem to be family devotions and church attendance.

Family devotions. Family altars may become a means for imposing religious aggression upon family members. In the evangelical tradition nearly all family counselors and church ministers argue for the need to establish a family altar. The accent is sufficiently strong that virtually all church families who do not maintain devotions together experience guilt and evade discussion about the matter. Furthermore, the pattern of a family altar has usually been presented in a rigid formula—stipulated Bible reading and repetitive prayer. This leads to a lack of creativity, variety and appeal. Devotions are sometimes discussed in the context of a pre-twentieth century life pattern, making them difficult to practice for a family living within a modern time schedule. But the problem can be solved. Family devotions are possible and can be attractive. They require creative approaches.

Church attendance. At some point during the rearing of children, most parents are confronted with rebellion against churchgoing. At first parents prevail by insisting on church attendance. Children are taken to Sunday School and church in spite of their protest and grousing. Eventually, however, compulsion appears to be counterproductive. If they have been forced to attend, children may later use this compulsion to rationalize their neglect of church.

Some early difficulties may relate to the church selected by the parents. If my children agreed to attend a church other than my choice, a church in which they could mature as Christians, I would agree to change churches. I would not insist upon their attendance with me as long as they found a fellowship in which they could advance their own Christian experience. I would release them to attend the church of their choice. The family togetherness concept, as commendable and pleasant as it is, should not be allowed to hinder a child's spiritual growth. Loyalty to a weak or declining church is not a virtue when the spiritual welfare of my children is in question.

How Our Family Coped with Religious Aggression

What are some of the solutions to the problems caused by religious aggression? Those who hold authority in families must permit rights of individualism in matters of spiritual experience. Christianity does not encourage slavish responses to authority. If Michal had retained her formal approach and David his casual style, they could have accepted one another and left the results to God. It is common to see a refined and genteel lady married to a man who is unaware of the niceties of appropriate manners, language and grooming. It is possible to develop a marriage style where each permits the other to become what that person, under God, wishes to become.

Children must become themselves, not cookie-cutter images of their parents. The parents' duty is to provide guidance and an environment in which the child may discover himself and develop at his own pace. One Mother's Day, our younger daughter, in her eighteenth year, gave her mother a gift. The gift was a piece of paper with Psalm 18:36 printed on it: "Thou givest me room for my steps; my feet have not faltered." Although the verse refers to God's way of making room for each of those who will follow Him, our daughter wished to apply it on this day to her mother. The roominess God had given her, her mother had not taken away. Rather mother had enhanced her individuality—had seen to it that her personality would not be confined. She could make some of her own decisions and some of her own mistakes, and she could, without losing the love or confidence of her mother, take some turns her mother might not approve of.

When parents make boundaries, those limits are sometimes set too narrow and a child's personality is stunted. When there are no boundaries, the results may be more serious and create larger problems—fear, lack of direction, and a feeling in the child that he is not worth parental concern. A balance is possible. Our daughter, on that Mother's Day, felt her mother had provided that balance between freedom and limitation.

A marriage partner should not impose his pattern of spiritual life on his mate. Both persons should strive for understanding and tolerance. Then both must leave the matter to the judgment of God. The greater the understanding that exists between members in the family, the easier is the task of family development and the less one feels inclined to play God with his children. Each member of the family owes every other member understanding and the kind of behavior that is motivated by it. Understanding does not necessarily mean approval of attitudes or acts.

As children reach an accountable age, they must, more and more, take responsibility for their behavior. They should learn to function as mature persons with integrity. This was my assumption in rearing young children: If my position was justifiable, my explanations were clear, and my motives were acceptable, my children would make the right decision. At some point I had to trust them. Lack of trust usually meant that my own position was weak or inadequately expressed.

Our family devotions. The differences my wife and I had relative to family devotions emerged soon after we were married. I determined to have devotions in the pattern which ministers and teachers tended to recommend—a time set aside for all members of the family to engage in Bible reading and prayer. I launched the program at the outset of our marriage without any review with my wife. Within a few weeks I could sense that my approach was not succeeding in its purpose. I noticed that she was bored and uneasy about our devotions.

I asked one evening after I had begun to read aloud, "You don't care for this, do you?"

"No." The answer was matter of fact. She was not harsh.

"Why not?" I felt somewhat uneasy.

"My father always insisted on his repetitious, sometimes long devotions, even when everything was going wrong in the family. They were always the same. I suppose we children rebelled because of his attitude as well as from boredom. At times dad would yell at us to get things started. Little seemed to be really spiritual or meaningful to us. The girls kept silent but the boys made no bones about their feelings. The day arrived when I hated devotions."

It took me several days to appreciate fully the depth of her feeling. At first I was deeply disappointed. I must have failed; she must have failed. At length I replied, "Let us have our devotions separately. And let us leave all this with the Lord to work out."

Not much happened at first. We were in the ministry —helping people and encouraging them to have family altars. I wonder if my counsel sustained much conviction. However, our ministry showed evidence of God's blessing.

Our children were born. Both my wife and I believed they should have spiritual guidance that would in part emerge from devotional experiences. The matter was largely left to me, although when I traveled my wife took on the parental duty. I started, haltingly. I prayed daily with our first child until the day came when she, like her mother, said she would like to develop her own devotionals. She was a private type of person and she became quiet but firm in her faith and practice.

At first I prayed separately with our sons. Then the boys developed an informal approach. I was expected to join them in devotions. One of us would read and one would pray. I did either or both only if requested by our sons to do so. Often there would be questions, with 15-minute discussions following. The atmosphere was open and free. If devotions could be said to be masculine in style and format, we had masculine devotions. I recall them with nostalgia and thanksgiving to God.

From an adult's point of view, the most humorous yet poignant experiences were the devotional periods I shared with our younger daughter. For about two years she turned each devotional into a full church service. We included everything but announcements and offering. She selected one or two hymns in advance and marked the places with slips of paper. We read one of the responsive readings; she haltingly read the bold print and I the small. We then read from the Bible, and she usually chose an entire chapter or more. This would lead to questions. Then both of us prayed. Seldom did I escape the room in less than 15 minutes—a half-hour was common. I recall those periods with a great deal of emotion and long to recreate one of those glowing half-hours when, lounging on her bed with her head and shoulders cradled on my left arm and chest, we sang and talked and read and prayed.

The years have fled from us. The children are grown and they now find their own patterns for Christian development. For the most part, we are gratified. Each claims to be God's child. Only the youngest is unmarried. We are grandparents. My wife and I can pray together now because we have found spontaneity which is totally separated from her unhappy childhood experiences. She developed her own devotional life and began to share with me. I took texts and ideas that she discovered and enlarged them for my own ministry and preaching. We found our way and refused to permit a dogmatic viewpoint to enslave us or spoil either our personal or spiritual lives. It was a creative approach that encouraged spiritual devotion in a family that did not follow stereotypes.

Our church attendance. Church membership and attendance were also problems for us. The issues in our lives were similar to those faced by families we counseled. As our family grew older, our children dispersed to different congregations. My work, involving travel to speaking points near and far, caused a strain, but we were able to weather those circumstances by accepting one another and respecting each other's wishes.

We did go through a short period when one of our sons did not wish to attend church. It was while we were attending our home church together. We met the challenge in a way many would consider unsatisfactory. Our younger son announced that he did not plan to go to church one Sunday morning. He was firm and straightforward. I could have insisted on my own way. He would have been obedient. Perhaps that is the reason I did not choose that option. He had always been obedient and had exhibited satisfactory attitudes. I agreed that he could remain at home, but he could not watch television or play outside. He could read or rest, but nothing more. He accepted the terms. None of the other children protested, nor did they change their own conduct. My wife was distressed and so, secretly, was I.

This pattern continued each Sunday for five weeks. On the sixth Sunday and without announcement the boy prepared for church and rejoined the family in worship. During the afternoon I asked why he had absented himself and why he had begun again. He said that God had permitted him to make his own decision to become a Christian and he hoped his father would as well. Although his logic escapes me, I am satisfied that our response was successful. It worked.

I remain uncertain about the principle that guided my strategy in that situation. We refused to make a major issue of the affair and it dissolved. Our view has been that deep love and gentle but firm discussion would help us through problems even if some of our decisions could be questioned. The process was successful in solving this problem. It was creative for us.

Whose Church Shall We Join?

At the outset of marriage, which church or which denomination should we join? Shall we join his? Hers? Some other?

Church membership can become a major issue in a marriage. It may seem unimportant at the outset of a marriage but it usually becomes more important later on. This is a key factor to be faced by Catholics and non-Catholics in marriages, although not so intense a problem as it once was. And some Protestant denominations maintain barriers against each other that seem even more formidable than the traditional Catholic/non-Catholic tensions in mixed marriage.

I was once invited to assist in a counseling session between a young man from a very formal liturgical church with Calvinistic background and a young woman from a charismatic Arminian tradition. It became clear that the future of the couple would be full of pitfalls, although both man and woman were clearly Christian in their faith. The discovery of an acceptable church home would become difficult. It is doubtful that either parental church would serve the couple.

In a Catholic/non-Catholic situation the problem may be confused somewhat by the fact that the two parties differ in the degree of their commitment. But after the birth of a child the flagging faith of one member may revive. Although not interested in church for himself, he develops a high degree of concern over the religious identity of his child. The other partner, believing that the mate had lapsed in church interest, felt capable of coping with the situation existing before the child's arrival. Permitted to continue his or her own practice of faith, he fully planned to include the child. Suddenly the religiously active mate confronts this unexpected barrier. The consequent tension may become severe and lead to divorce.

Differences in doctrine that spouses allow between themselves may prove serious sources of tension after children are added to the family unit. For example, marital tension became severe for a particular couple facing baptism or dedication options for their children. One mate was very firm in the belief that child baptism is necessary to provide assurance of eternal safety for children in the event of premature death. The other believed that baptism is a sign or ordinance that must be chosen by an individual after his conversion and that infant baptism is an act of superstition. The resolution of differences was not easy to arrive at for this husband and wife, feeling as intensely as each one did about the matter. They never fully resolved the conflict.

Differences sometimes become sufficiently intense to cause husband and wife to reject all church affiliations. They distort issues beyond reasonable dimensions. These issues are sometimes used as excuses to escape responsibility. Finding fault with the church does not remove one's responsibility to relate to the church, even as criticizing the government does not free one from his duties to that government. Persons whose religious commitments are not strong will design rationalizations for evading church attendance. There is a place for each believer in an organized church. He is obligated to find it. Those Christians who do not go to church, even if they "read the Bible and pray at home," tend to be underdeveloped Christians. Generally, they are unhappy and unable to show that their private Bible reading has satisfied their real needs. And as Anatole France remarked somewhere in his writings: Unhappiness makes people look stupid. Perhaps the unhappy person will also act stupidly.

How a Family May Resolve Conflicts on Church

Recognizing the preeminence of Christ is the foremost responsibility of the Christian. Church membership is important to the development of a Christian life, but one's personal experience of Christ is even more basic and important. When Christ holds an appropriate place in the life of a person, he becomes an instrument for improving the ministry of the church with which he identifies.

There usually is a local church that will fit the personality of a given family and at the same time provide spiritual sustenance. A young woman of my acquaintance is married to a man who is not a Christian. Her affinity is for an intensely evangelical church affiliated with an avowed fundamental denomination. The husband, however, doesn't agree.

They invested weeks discussing the problem, both openly reviewing their feelings. She agreed to attend a specific church of a large, more formal denomination. That particular church is evangelical, though following a somewhat more sophisticated pattern of ministry than she was used to. Her husband joined her in the new venture. The wife is maturing and contributing as a Christian, and her husband is displaying the usual preliminary responses that lead to personal commitment. I predict success for both of them.

Husband and wife ought to yield on various points, at the same time guarding the convictions of both parties. For the couple differing on baptism, the mate opposing infant baptism might yield, with the understanding that he would be allowed to express his views to the child at appropriate times in future years. If this was done in love and without rancor toward the mate, the maturing child would be able to make up his own mind. If the arguments seemed persuasive, the young adult would likely submit to another baptismal experience as an expression of personal faith.

The Christian faith is meant to be liberating. When it appears as something that limits, that distorts, that robs men of joyful life, understanding and freedom, it is not true Christianity. It is a religion created out of human culture, opinions and prejudices. Biblical Christianity has within it the resources that will enable faithful believers to solve problems.

PART THREE
INTIMACY

Defraud ye not one the other. (1 Cor. 7:5)

CHAPTER SIX

SEXUAL FRUSTRATION IN MARRIAGE

Key points in this chapter include:
- what is a happy marriage
- how sexual activity relates to nonverbal communication
- why sexual differences may cause major discord
- what is really known about sex
- what are some problems of sexual intimacy without marriage.
- what are male and female differences in sexuality
- what distortions of sex are doing to Christians
- how attitudes about sex change between generations

Now concerning the things whereof ye wrote unto me: It is good for a man not to touch a woman. Nevertheless, to avoid fornication, let every man have his own wife, and let every woman have her own husband. Let the husband render unto the wife due benevolence: and likewise also the wife unto the husband. The wife hath not power of her own body, but the husband: and likewise also the husband hath not power of his own body, but the wife. Defraud ye not one the other, except it be with consent for a time, that ye may give yourselves to fasting and prayer; and come together again, that Satan tempt you not for your incontinency. (1 Cor. 7:1-5)

Problems encountered by counselors are generally grouped for study. But we err if we treat them in stereotyped ways. Each couple provides new insights into marriage and marriage problems. Among generalized groups of problems, those that are sex-related are particularly individualistic. They are intensely personal and seem unique to each troubled couple. In *Anna Karenina*, Leo Tolstoy captured this truth in his observation: "All happy families resemble one another; every unhappy family is unhappy in its own way."

The Anatomy of a Happy Marriage
A successful marriage is not easily analyzed. No special pattern for happy marriages can be generalized. Analysts meet only with troubled couples and tend to build their theories from families that fail. A description of a happy marriage is less dramatic than that of a failing one. Two persons live for each other, accept one another

and celebrate life as they find it. Their expectations are realistic to human nature. They work out family goals and values. They know that mutual appreciation and affirmation contribute to marital success. Individual peculiarities are not magnified out of proportion. Intimacy is assumed to be a natural and necessary part of the relationship.

Reviews of happy marriages show that these husbands and wives have faced and worked through serious marital problems. They may have had grounds for divorce, but rejected the option. They believed in their ability to win. The causes for success could be found in the character of the persons themselves.

Other couples failed even when their situations were conducive to achievement. Marriage as an institution is not to be commended if the couple succeeds, nor to be faulted if the couple fails in the relationship. Lloyd Ogilvie summarizes the point: "There are no problem marriages: there are problem people who are married to each other."

Lists of reasons accounting for the collapse of marriages are often published. Couples in the process of seeking marital counsel or turning to divorce courts cite the standard problems. Disagreements about money, nagging and disregard of one's person by the other are high on the lists. Communication breakdown and sexual conflicts are common causes of failure, although they are not named as high priority complaints as often as one might expect. Sex and communication problems generally are mixed with other matters. For example, nagging is a communication problem, even though the sender or receiver may not recognize it as such.

Sex Begins with Nonverbal Communication

Complaints in the area of sexual activity may be

closely related to communication problems, although this is seldom perceived by the troubled couple. In time and with appropriate counsel a couple may expect to identify and understand the nonverbal behavior that has much to do with satisfaction in marital intimacy. Words are important and reinforce sexual experience. But nonverbal communication provides a more direct depth experience than words can provide.

A glance of the eye, a turn of the lips, a sincere gesture, or one withheld—these express intense meaning. Clever persons may fake them but not indefinitely. In sex, aggression or nonaggression, animation or nonanimation, attitudes, openness, grooming, and acceptance of one's own sexuality are more forceful in intimate communication than words. Couples can learn to identify these nonverbal ways of communicating acceptance or rejection and, with perception, improve their sending and receiving of "messages."

Where there is love and acceptance between husband and wife, "making love" poses no great problem. Happy marriages appear unified in their intimacy. But unhappy marriages seem to be made up of fragments as confusing as a giant, complex jigsaw puzzle. A counselor may expect that a majority of the couples he confronts find sexual differences and interests to be major discord factors. Dr. Joyce Brothers summarized the statistics: "It is believed that half of all marriages in the United States are troubled by some type of sexual problem."[1] The opinion polls that place sex rather far down on the list of marital aggravations seem to be contradicted by the actual experiences of counselors. Evidently, in these polls sexual problems are hidden beneath other issues that can more comfortably be discussed.

Sexual interest and activity often come up in counseling sessions as an outgrowth of a discussion of some other issue. When the other issue is solved, sexual adjustment often follows even if the subject of sex is not treated in depth. Persons troubled about money, or insensitivity, or about some other matter, will often express their wrath to their mates by denial or misuse of sex. Adjust the finances or mend insensitive attitudes and intimacy is restored. The subject of sex itself should neither be handled as a hush-hush issue, nor should it be treated as nearly the total meaning of marriage, as it sometimes is.

Aroused awareness of one's own sexuality is a common personal need in marriage. Sex awareness groups may take undue advantage of this human need. Joseph Epstein, the eminent editor of *The American Scholar*, wrote a book on broken marriage, entitled *Divorced in America*. He asked the question, "What part does sex have in the breakup of marriage?" He was critical of the "sexologists" who snigger about "funsex." He wrote:

> Nerve centers, glands, protuberances, engorgements, contractions. The sexologists do not talk about human behavior but instead about the behavior of the sexual apparatus. Such qualities as privacy, modesty, shame, fidelity fall outside the realm of their discussion, having long ago been replaced by such terms as foreplay, forepleasure, high frequency impulses, ejaculation. Sex becomes, as Aldous Huxley once described it, "a maniac struggling in the musky darkness with another maniac."[2]

Sex Is More than Plumbing

Failure in sexual intimacy often is a result of unrealistic expectations on the part of one or both partners. An attitude has emerged from the emphasis on sexual technique that any failure to reach erotic expectations can be solved in a mechanical way. Discussions in popular literature often concentrate on sexual athletics. Sexual organs become pieces of equipment by which new records of performance may be set. David Hubbard reminds us that "Sex is more than plumbing."

According to the eminent psychiatrist, Rollo May, the prevalent popular attitude leads to "alienation, feelings of loneliness and depersonalization." Amitai Etzioni, Columbia University sociologist, contended: "Increasingly the separation of sex from affection is being discovered by the avant-garde as a pathway to frustration, tension and jealousy. The movement of American society toward reducing sex to animal-like conduct between people is about to end. People are seeking ways to draw a line between sexual freedom and sexual frenzy."[3]

One of the dilemmas of our time is the contradiction between the available volume of information on sex and the prevailing public ignorance about the subject. The reason is that a large percentage of the "information" available is really misinformation.

Take, for example, the matter of premarital sex and its consequences. With significant exceptions, secular literature commonly accepts premarital sex as appropriate, even necessary, conduct. The implication is that a person will learn about his or her sexual capabilities through encounters with one or more persons. Furthermore, premarital sexual experiences are supposed to provide evidence of the possibility for marriage success or failure between two persons. As the argument goes, one would not purchase a pair of shoes without trying them on. The analogy is a poor one, but it is attractive to those seeking justification for easy sexual liaison. This is not a new philosophy. Many couples in every generation have followed the same pattern. The only difference is that today the practice is afforded some public approval and therefore is more widespread.

Sexual Tryouts Are Not the Answer

Persons who recommend sexual tryouts disregard a considerable body of information that is known about sexual activity and attitudes both in and out of marriage. Approaching a sample of 15- to 21-year-olds, a Louis Harris poll in 1970 asked the question: "Will sexual experience before marriage contribute to happiness later?" Only one in four respondents thought it would. That means that a majority of those who most immediately faced the issue doubted the popularized view.

Dr. Seymour Halleck, writing in *Parent's Magazine*, stated: "Permissive sexual activity seems to be highly correlated with mental illness." And Dr. Herbert J. Miles wrote: "I checked my personal marriage counseling files and found that 76 percent of the cases involved premarital sex relations as part of the total problem of the marriage conflict."

Advocates of premarital sex imply an unproved and, I believe, false premise that effectual sexual relationship is the primary factor in creating a happy marriage. A satisfying premarital sex pattern often dissolves into a different pattern within a matter of a few weeks or months after marriage. Some of the troubled married couples I have counseled had earlier succeeded through premarital sexual experiences to establish a belief in their compatibility. Encouraged by this, they married, only to find that they had deeper adjustment problems.

I am convinced by my experience as a counselor that successful premarital experiences offer little assurance of later happiness whether the man and woman marry or not. I have been informed by counselees, "Before and right after marriage we had lots of sex, now we have none at all." They want to know what went wrong. In most instances the partners had gradually changed in their behavior toward one another. John Scanzoni rightly pointed out: "Persons ... tend to overlook the fact that no matter what bargain a couple strike at marriage —whether there has been a trial or not—*change* inevitably occurs."

Whatever gratification an unmarried but cohabiting couple may achieve, they usually pay a high price in negative experiences. It is common for guilt and fear to dominate and health problems often arise. Sexual intimacy often becomes the area for frustration and insecurity. If one member has had several partners, the current partner is sometimes called upon to meet or surpass others in performance. Both men and women have complained in counseling sessions that a present partner "is not as good as" another, or that "this other one made me feel better."

For married couples who move on to higher ideals, the fact that virginity was lost before marriage to a person other than one's mate may create a later emotional problem. Even though it is made to appear old-fashioned in modern society, maintenance of virginity before marriage continues to possess meaning and beauty. There is value in the concept that one saves that gift for the one beloved, even before the beloved is known. It is a gift that can only be given once. There is no second chance. If virginity has no continuing significance, why is it that even crude and unprincipled persons attach importance to sexual encounter with virgins? There is a mystery to the first sexual experience. No one ever forgets the beginning of that intimacy if it includes intercourse.

Preoccupation with sex prevents unmarried couples

from dealing with the other vital issues that will have to be faced if their relationships continue. Children, money matters, security for the family, long-range plans, and other important issues are seldom discussed and settled. After a short time of cohabiting, unmarried couples find themselves embroiled in differences similar to those encountered by marrieds. Their chances of surviving problems are poorer because without marriage they do not have the commitment required to solve conflicts. So one member may abandon the other or a mutual breakup may occur. If marriage encounters problems in modern society, cohabitation without marriage presents even more difficulties.

Although most unmarried cohabiting couples do not admit sexual incompatibility (which would be an admission of failure for their life-style), they commonly separate from one another. Man and woman may drift from partner to partner for several years until, partly exhausted, partly disillusioned, they choose marriage. They see it as their final hope for developing maturity, settling down, finding permanent values and satisfying inner urges to develop more than the sexual dimensions of relationship. Self-respect, children, sexual satisfaction (more than gratification), social approval, tenderness, security, trust and faith, are seldom, if ever, found in satisfactory balance outside of marriage.

I have never observed a sense of lasting fulfillment in a couple outside of marriage, although there appeared to be promise during the first months of some relationships. One searches long to find a casual relationship that is old. There may be some successful liaisons which are ongoing. The eminent French couple of literary fame, Jean Paul Sartre and Simone de Beauvoir, are commonly cited, but few others. Why are there not other effective examples among millions of couples in the earth's population? Because the main ingredient to a relationship of marriage, love with responsibility, must always be in short supply in casual liaison. The probabilities of success are against unmarried couples. Evidence is unpromising for a happy and lifelong experience of loyalty and love without marriage.

One of the reasons for avoiding premarital sexual intercourse is that it is best for mates to learn about intimacy together, without the imposition of other experiences into their relationship. Then no comparisons need be made to the performances of others. It is a sadly sensitive moment when a woman discusses in counseling sessions that she has been compared to others with whom her mate was intimate before marriage. What is a wife to say when her husband compares her figure with that of a woman with whom he had sexual relations before marriage? What will happen to either husband or wife when their sexual performance is rated lower than previous experiences with others? If premarital activity has taken place, it ought to be repented of and the memory of it dissolved.

Maleness and Femaleness

Maleness and femaleness are sexual expressions different in character and in intensity. It is common knowledge that the human male usually is more physically aggressive than the female, requires or seeks more sexual activity and responds more violently in physical climax. Predication on this is related to varying hormonal balances. Research on sex is not fully clear on how hormones function for either men or women. It is known that changes in hormonal balance will cause males to become female-like and females to become male-like. Nearly all sex changes are achieved by medical use of hormones and surgery.

During recent years women have been given greater recognition in sexual expression. The leaders in women's liberation argue in contradictory directions regarding sexuality of women. On the one hand some point out that sexual activity with men is demeaning to women and, even in marriage, constitutes rape. They suggest that after the birth of the woman's last child she would prefer to cease from sexual activity. On the other hand some boast that sexual interests of women are more dramatic, intense and fulfilling than those men can experience.

A man often achieves a climactic experience within a few minutes after initiating a sexual encounter, whereas a woman generally responds only after a longer period. One poll reported only nine percent of married women felt that their own sexual desire exceeded their husbands'. It is the general practice in our society that sexual activity is geared to meet the needs of the husband without sufficient regard for his wife. This situation often causes considerable tension. Misunderstanding and lack of adjustment between the sexes may also contribute to practices such as homosexuality and/or self-manipulation by either sex.

Other differences between the sexes are marked and may be troublesome. For example, an average young male in a marriage relationship will seek sexual contact with his wife in approximate 48- to 72-hour cycles. This is partly due to buildup of seminal fluids which he desires to expel and partly due to psychological needs. If an average husband does not experience contact in the two- to three-day cycle he becomes edgy. The wife more easily adjusts her cycles so that participation may be frequent or spasmodic as she chooses. Her responses appear to be unrelated to any fluid buildup, but they are closely related to her attitudes.

The majority of situations appear to be dictated by the pressing sexual needs of the husband. Consequently, most couples report a frequency of sexual intercourse of approximately three times weekly. Both happy and unhappy couples report the same time patterns. They generally do not know why they adopted the frequency. The wife's acceptance or rejection of the husband-dictated pattern may be meaningful in any analysis of a troubled marriage. A man may mentally overpower his sexual appetite and change his cycle of interest in order to improve his wife's satisfaction. If the new pattern is not unreasonable, his body will adjust to it.

As the movement for women's rights expanded there emerged a new problem for some men. Feeling threatened in their roles as aggressors, these men turned against sexual participation altogether. Some opt out of marriage. If they marry they may fear failure in performance and withdraw from sexual participation. Damage to their psyches probably occurred before marriage and has little or nothing to do with the women who have become their brides.

A man disinterested in sex who believes that women are also disinterested may marry in the assumption that few demands will be made on him. One young man refused to consummate a marriage even after several years of sympathetic love and patience exhibited by his wife. There was no physical impediment. The man did not see his own sexual function as a necessity for his marriage. The marriage was legally terminated. Both husband and wife were active Christians.

A man cannot pretend sexual gratification as easily as a woman can. Many women have maintained a charade of sexual enjoyment for a lifetime to please their husbands. A man and his alert wife know if he succeeds or fails. A man's anxiety over his sexual performance is compounded by the fact that even the fear of impotence can cause impotence. An increasing number of divorces, annulments and separations are occurring because of real or alleged male impotence. In their newfound freedom, with protection from pregnancy provided by abortion and birth control devices, many women are openly espousing increased interest and participation in sex. Women formerly muffled sexual desire because of the fear of pregnancy and a belief that passion was not virtuous in a woman.

Wife Swapping, Orgies and Taboos

The effect on the Christian community of the changing cultural milieu has been significant. Christian counselors, working with church people, are increasingly confronted with problems very similar to those reported in secular society. This is partly due to the fact that the church has been evasive on issues of sex in the lives of parishioners.

Old taboos die slowly, and one of these has been the much maligned Victorian attitude about sex. On the other hand, some church bodies and members have overcompensated in making adjustments. Many churches attempt to justify, and members to practice, permissive sex habits. Liberal and conservative denominations sometimes take varying approaches to the practice of sex in modern life. In their church communities, Christians have confronted and firmly rejected wife-swapping and orgies. Counselors do deal with common perversions among individual conservative Christians, but it appears that deviations are not widespread. Nevertheless, the church is currently faced with the problems of a membership which has been strongly influenced in sexual matters by a vast secular culture at odds with Christian values. Former church standards have moderated. In many cases the change represents decay in biblical standards.

As has been said, concern about pregnancy traditionally had much to do with female responsiveness, whereas the male felt little inhibition. During her fertile years a woman uses her ingenuity in order to avoid what she feels to be an excessive number of pregnancies. If she becomes obsessed with fear of pregnancy, that obsession will affect her sexual activity. Her husband may be unsympathetic because his experience is different from hers. Often there is little attempt by one mate to understand what the other must encounter physically or psychologically. Tensions result and each partner develops attitudes toward the other that influence or color other dimensions of their relationship.

Following the discovery of effective birth control methods, women's concern over unwanted pregnancy declined. Counselors discovered an abrupt reduction of pregnancy concerns as a problem in marriage. Surprisingly, the number of out-of-wedlock pregnancies remained high and, in some communities, increased. This was likely due to carelessness in utilizing birth control methods coupled with an increase in sexual activity.

Unfortunately, availability of preventive techniques may have encouraged increased sexual activity. Even in cases where preventives were not employed because of their inconvenience and cost, passionate youths believed their existence on the druggist's shelf carried magical properties. As a result unwanted pregnancies occurred and were sometimes terminated through clandestine or illegal abortions. In time the increase in the number of unwanted pregnancies among both marrieds and unmarrieds brought on the legalization of abortion. Legal abortions in America have been most often requested by married women who were mothers and did not wish to add to the size of their brood.

Most authorities contend that sexual activity within marriage has not changed markedly during the first three quarters of the twentieth century. The big change has been in sexual activity outside of marriage. Even so, there may be more change within marriage than available evidence reveals.

The Sexual Generation Gap

One of the main problems today is that mothers who faced issues different from those their daughters face may advise them as though the issues were similar. If a mother is persuaded that sex is dirty and pregnancy is to be feared, she will probably not be very effective in counseling her daughter who lives in an era when sex is accepted as a normal appetite and control of pregnancy is at hand. Parents need to become attentive to what has happened in a changing society. This does not imply that biblical concepts on sexual purity are to be diluted.

Ignorance on the subject of sex is appalling. It is important for parents and children alike to read extensively enough to sift out the dangerous from the useful in human sexual relations. Many excellent books provide useful sources for the Christian who is seeking help in understanding modern problems. Some of these are: *God, Sex and You: An Evangelical Perspective*, by M.O. Vincent; *I Married You*, by Walter Trobisch; *Christian: Celebrate Your Sexuality*, by Dwight Hervey Small; *The Act of Marriage*, by Tim and Beverly LaHaye; *Sex Is a Parent Affair*, by Letha Scanzoni.

For many years the subject of sex was not discussed or written about meaningfully by evangelical sources. But neither did secular sources treat the issues well. Much was written and talked about without being helpful to understanding and marriage solidarity.

Ministers and other Christians, serious students of human behavior, recognize the difficulties Christians face in solving problems of sexuality and intimacy in marriage. The unsatisfactory and contradictory advice found in secular literature—literature based on relativistic values—had to be countered by perceptions based on Christian values, revealed in the Scriptures.

Those Christian values affirm sexuality for men and women, rights and privileges of sexual activity in marriage, exclusiveness and spiritual meaning in fidelity to one partner, appropriateness of passion and desire within boundaries, and they affirm family generation in a love bond. So meaningful is Christian marriage that mates will maintain intimacy on a day-by-day basis until one member dies. Mates will be willing, if necessary, to abandon everyone except God for each other.

Sex and sexual relationships are God's inventions. God created from nothing—*ex nihilo*. To man, in man's perfect state, God gave the authority to do what He did—bring forth life. God created and man procreates. God lifted man out of dust. Man, through sexual union, continues that creative act. Whatever pleasure accrues in sexual relationships, it relates to spiritual meaning when it is cast in fidelity to biblical truths. To lift sexual practice and pleasure out of that context is to attempt to denigrate what God has done—and continues to do—for those who will follow His way.

Notes

1. *San Francisco Sunday Examiner and Chronicle*, April 18, 1976.
2. Joseph Epstein, "Report from the Sexual Revolution: Trouble at the 'Bedroom Olympics.'" *Reader's Digest* (March, 1975), p. 73.
3. *San Francisco Chronicle*, February 2, 1975.

CHAPTER SEVEN

SEXUAL LIBERATION IN MARRIAGE

Key points in this chapter include:
- how sexual sin is to be treated
- what causes the decline in sexual intimacy for married couples
- what is the state of the public knowledge about sex
- what are some common problems in marriage intimacy
- how to find a balanced sexual experience in marriage

And Isaac dwelt in Gerar: And the men of the place asked him of his wife; and he said, She is my sister: for he feared to say, She is my wife; lest, said he, the men of the place should kill me for Rebekah; because she was fair to look upon. And it came to pass, when he had been there a long time, that Abimelech king of the Philistines looked out at a window, and saw, and, behold, Isaac was sporting with Rebekah his wife. And Abimelech called Isaac, and said, Behold, of a surety she is thy wife: and how saidst thou, She is my sister? And Isaac said unto him, Because I said, Lest I die for her. And Abimelech said, What is this thou hast done unto us? One of the people might lightly have lain with thy wife, and thou shouldest have brought guiltiness upon us. And Abimelech charged all his people, saying, He that toucheth this man or his wife shall surely be put to death. (Gen. 26:6-11)

Our parents and friends help create in us a sense of right and wrong. The standards they impart to us may be satisfactory or unsatisfactory depending upon their own orientation. Historically, the Christian society has looked upon sexual sins as among the worst kinds. A murderer might expect to find forgiveness among Christians more readily than an adulterer.

Every sin is evil. And every sin may be forgiven by God through human repentance and the divine sacrifice of Christ. Sexual sin should be treated by Christians just as are thievery, hatred, gossip or any other spiritual failure—by sincere confession, forgiveness and a genuine commitment to righteousness. Some Christians feel they have not sinned seriously if they have not deviated in sexual purity, but if they failed in this area they feel they have forfeited their chances for effective service the rest of their lives. Such intense attitudes tend to make sexual activity even in marriage relationships seem somewhat tainted. Parents, hoping to keep their child virginal, may create an attitude about sex in the child that will make him or her an unhappy spouse in adult life. Questionable advice may be given to sons and daughters by parents seeking to keep down their children's sexual expression. Such approaches by parents are more likely to leave a lasting effect on daughters than on sons, although sons are certainly affected as well. Physical pressures in young men often make the repressions of parents and society seem unrealistic. They are more likely than their sisters to rebel openly.

Furthermore, much of the Christian community's idealism about sex and personal righteousness may be lip service that does not translate into individual lives. Somewhere between total repression and unrestrained license there is a balance of legitimate sexuality. The Christian is driven back to the Scriptures to find that balance. There he finds guiding principles and significant examples of the results in the lives of persons who disregarded the principles.

Queen Victoria's Sexual Prudery

Concentration on the sinfulness of some sexual thought or activity may stem from the strong influence of Victorianism upon the church. Queen Victoria was the reigning monarch of England for much of the nineteenth century. Her husband, Prince Albert, died when Victoria was in mid-life and she lived nearly 40 years as a widow. She was the most prominent female influence on the culture of the western world during the nineteenth century, leaving a heritage of sexual prudery to all English-speaking peoples. Conservative Christians before this time, like the Puritans of New England, neither taught nor practiced "Victorian" prudery, although they are sometimes blamed for it.

The effect of the Victorian influence was to label sex as dirty and acceptable only as means for reproduction. It is not entirely clear why the church accepted this viewpoint. Many religious leaders taught that it had biblical sanction and it quickly became part of the "Christian" message. Women presumed that Victoria, a good woman, was their proper example. The result has been unfortunate, a repressive influence on marital intimacy and happiness. Many of the distortions continue to cloud the issues related to sexuality.

It is disillusioning to discover how many persons are immature, even cruel, in their physical and emotional manipulation of others. Often a woman uses sex as her means of rewarding or punishing her husband. And it is not uncommon for one partner either to reduce sexual activity dramatically or to turn away gradually so that by middle age, a psychological sexual impotence is achieved in the other mate.

Causes of Mid-Forties Impotency

Psychological impotence is common in men in their mid-forties. Their wives have resisted a normal pattern of physical intimacy. These husbands felt rejected and retreated from activity or argument. However, the same wives, now older women, sense in themselves an increasing store of hormones. They are past fertility and their children are reared. They wish to revive intimate relationship.

The husband, "turned off" during earlier years, may now be psychologically incapable of performance. He

102

may require considerable assistance through counseling if he is to resume participation. Male ego may prevent him from seeking help. Having been forced to abstain, he found a compromise or learned abstinence. He is unwilling to reopen the subject. If he did make an attempt and failed, his masculinity might come into question. He will not risk that. He reminds his wife that it was she who terminated the activity some years before, and that is the way it should remain. She is to blame. He may never forgive her and, in various ways, generally by sullen silence, may punish her for the years of denial.

Failure of sexual activity in marriage between physically normal mates may be traced to a number of causes.

Poor information or lack of information may contribute to impotency. It might be expected that with greater openness about sex, widespread dissemination of printed and visual media dealing with every aspect of sexual activity, and more formal sex education than has ever been attempted, the population would be well informed about sex. A 1976 youth poll, taken from a significant sample of American boys and girls from all states of the union, shows the opposite to be true. Gordon Sabine reported on the poll:

> Not more than 1 percent said they learned from their mothers. About 10 percent said sex education classes in school were helpful. About a third said they learned from movies, "bathroom walls," and "dirty magazines." More than half said they learned from other students, "most of whom don't know what they're talking about."

> Youthpoll America discovered that there is no reliable, organized source of sex information. The talk that goes around, the dirty

jokes, the bragging about exploits, the "facts" sometimes turned around so they're exactly backward, all add up to a national problem— even a tragedy.[1]

Sabine also revealed that most boys said they gained their sex information "by listening to older boys talking and by looking at pictures in 'adult' magazines in drug-stores."

Other recent studies show that abysmal ignorance about sex remains and that the greater dissemination of information (or misinformation) has served only to arouse the population to frenzied sexual activity. This has most likely contributed to the increase in premarital sex, in fatherless babies, in the incidence of venereal disease. Sabine said that in 1975 "the United States [experienced] an estimated 250,000 unplanned, unwed teen-age pregnancies." Some reports estimate even higher numbers.

Useful information is sometimes lost in the sea of pornography that floods the population like a tide. Some conscientious persons may avoid reading appropriate books on sex because of the sleazy reputation that sex literature has gained. Trashy books and magazines are circulated with a tongue-in-cheek claim that they serve a social need ("redeeming social value") and provide clinical information. Physicians and counselors know that pornographic books and magazines do not fulfill any need except one that they create. Having aroused prurient interest, the publications then attempt to satisfy that interest. The process is circular.

It is sometimes argued that pornography is useful as a means of releasing in troubled persons sexual urges that might otherwise result in negative aggressive action. An analogy has been found in drugs. When an addict goes through withdrawal, he may be placed on prescription drugs. He requires drugs to moderate his drug abuse. But the analogy does not hold up. There is nothing here comparable to physical withdrawal from drugs. If pornography is needed to control persons with strong sex drives, it must be asked what in the person's environment generated the excessive drives in the first place? Why do men dominate the readership of pornographic materials? Why has sexual aggression upon innocents increased during the era when pornography has been freely available? And if an outlet is required, is there no better way? Must the sexoholic be condemned to a lifetime of feeding his mind on the product of this sordid industry?

Distortion of sex by parents or others, may be another cause for impotency. Although Christian youths have often received questionable or limited advice about sex, it appears the guidance is at least as good as that commonly provided by non-Christian parents and sources. A survey by *Redbook* concluded that religiously-oriented women enjoy sexual relations more than nonreligious women. The poll showed highest satisfaction among those who considered themselves "strongly religious"; "moderately religious" were less gratified, and nonreligious least so.[2]

One commentator argued that the taint of sin in sexual activity creates titillation that gratifies religious persons.[3] But this interpretation is contrary to other evidence. The excitement of premarital relations reported by Christians and non-Christians alike is often lost after marriage. The loss appears to be even between the two groups, and guilt that follows appears more severe for religious women. Guilt, if anything, reduces sexual activity. Counselors commonly encounter complaints, principally from women, that attractive forbidden fruit before marriage appears unattractive afterwards. So a marriage built around the excitement of "sinful" sex is likely to be unhappy, rather than satisfying.

Before the *Redbook* study, longtime speculation held that religious faith and sexual repression went hand in hand. When evidence showed that religious women were less repressed than the nonreligious, the critics made a fast shuffle. They suggested that because religious women would relate sex with sin they would enjoy intimacy more than their nonreligious sisters. What does religion do—create repression or gratification? It appears to have never occurred to those detractors that God invented sex, removed guilt from it in Christian marriage, and has delivered its best experience to persons who feel spiritual bonding in sexual unity.

Even studies of the elderly show that religious persons are likely to be more sexually active. Among males of advanced age who have worked as professionals, clergymen are sexually most active.[4] The presently available evidence for sexual gratification and compatibility highly favors Christian husbands and wives.

In advising their children, Christians have often been accused of making sex appear dirty. There is a sense in which secularists are even more likely to treat the subject in that way. The non-Christian may be preoccupied with prurient interests. He supports a considerable industry trafficking in sex. He sniggers at a sexually suggestive idea or joke. Sex embarrasses him, hence he may flaunt it to escape personal discomfort. Sydney J. Harris discussed the contrast with other peoples: "There are numerous societies we call 'primitive' where a dirty story would not be understood, much less appreciated, because sex is not a subject for titillation any more than breathing or eating."

There is no evidence that Christians have experienced greater failure than non-Christians in sexual guidance of youth. On the other hand, there is some evidence that they have done a somewhat better job.

Couples may have unrealistic sexual expectations. The claims and implications of much pornographic literature are simply untrue. Sexual athletes are very rare. And certain physical limitations are obvious. A male cannot manufacture seminal fluids as rapidly as many pornographic stories would require. So multitudes of persons are reading books and attempting to emulate conduct that is impossible for all but a very few persons, if any. No one can achieve all the fantasies. Even if it were possible to act out the alleged behavior, it would not provide the gratification that is claimed for it.

A good deal of sordidness currently passes for legitimate sexual activity. Christian counselors work with couples who were fairly compatible until they read books that promised them previously unknown intimacies and joys. Not being able to experience the hoped-for ecstasies, the couples feel inadequate and troubled. They begin to doubt their relationships. This problem of distorted expectations is summarized by Ruth Winter: "The major problem with marriage concerns false expectations. Young people don't realize that someone has to change the baby's diaper and take out the garbage. They don't know that no human is always in a good mood; everyone's feelings get hurt; few women look beautiful in the morning, and that not all men are as eager and ever ready for sex as *Playboy* would have us believe."[5]

Some couples may become bored with mechanical methods. Human beings resent boredom, yet they seldom exert themselves to make the changes that would give them full satisfaction in their experiences. Sexual activity could be effectively varied within the limits of good taste. Most persons do not bother. They have a repetitious and mechanical approach to this sacred relationship. But redundancy in sex is not necessary. While it may be harmful to attempt to follow exotic patterns publicized in some technique books, couples ought to use their own imaginations to bring tenderness, variety and affection into sexual relationships. No set frequency of contact between husband and wife nor any other concept about sexual practice should be imposed by the experience of others.

The problem of boredom generally stems from wrong attitudes and ignorance. For example, in the United States the common position for husband and wife to take in the marriage act is for the wife to rest on her back with her husband above her. Many couples never attempt any break with that pattern. Some women state that the suggestions of their husbands for a change of position seemed immoral to them. Yet this position is considered strange in other culture. It has become known as "the missionary position" because native peoples intercepted missionaries in their intimacy and were intrigued by the American custom. In a number of countries the people mock the common American approach and consider it unsatisfactory sexual practice. There is nothing natural or Christian about one position or practice over another. Sexual variety within the bond of marriage is highly recommended as a means for reducing boredom.

A couple's unwillingness to talk about sexual intimacy may lead to impotency. It is common for a person to assume that his spouse knows his sexual desires and expectations. But it is impossible for a person, no matter how sincerely he and his partner relate to one another, to guess with accuracy what the other is thinking. Some persons are mute even to their mates when it comes to sexual intimacy. Unwillingness or inability to talk about

108

one's hopes and limitations will almost certainly lead to disappointment and misunderstanding. For example, when a husband does not guess precisely what is wanted, the wife assumes that he is unloving, thoughtless and inconsiderate. This guessing game in marriage is responsible for considerable grief. If we do not learn to verbalize our expectations we should accept in good grace whatever comes to us.

Sex Is Fragile—Handle with Care

A belief in the sanctity of appropriate sex is necessary. What God has given should not be distorted. In the marriage bond sexual relationships are God-given and blessed. A biblically-based, sexual relationship may provide the most dynamic human encounter and experience possible.

The Bible provides extensive and explicit information about sex and marriage. The apostle Paul, whom one might expect to avoid the whole subject because of his own status as a bachelor, acknowledged as natural the expectations and intimacy of marriage (see 1 Cor. 7). He taught that each mate had sexual rights with the other, that there should be no physical withdrawal from each other, even for a night, without a mutual decision to do so for designated spiritual reasons. The marriage act is touted as natural and valuable in itself apart from procreation.

A particularly sensitive passage in the Old Testament provides a glimpse into the private lives of Isaac and Rebekah (Gen. 26:6-12). Believing that the men of Gerar might kill him in order to take his wife, Isaac lied and announced that she was his sister. The ruse appeared to be working. However, Abimelech the king, looking out from a window, saw that "Isaac was sporting with Rebekah his wife." In a slang term, they were "necking."

One translation uses "caressing." Abimelech believed that a brother and sister would not conduct themselves as Isaac and Rebekah were doing. Isaac's and Rebekah's sexual desires became sufficiently strong that they accepted the risk of the garden meeting—for sexual encounter. Abimelech understood the needs of a couple but he reprimanded Isaac for his misrepresentation. Nearly four millennia have passed and human desire, given of God, continues to demand similar attention.

The Song of Solomon, the Proverbs, and other biblical passages affirm the sensuous nature of man and woman. The sexual interests of those ancient writers may be equated with our interests. Human nature is basically unchanged. Therefore these writings are relevant today. God has created man with a prowess toward woman. In this way sexuality finds its fulfillment. Understanding that relationship and its boundaries is a primary matter for mature persons. Successful marriage is built in part on this understanding.

The biblical ideal is one man with one woman. Adam was totally identified with Eve. That ideal was referred to in various biblical statements. The principle of having a single partner with whom one learns and develops a pattern of intimacy is logically sound. Why should any person need more than one living mate?

Control Sexual Appetite with Love

The unlimited rule of love should guide marital duties and privileges. Love will allow the needs of both partners to be met and will consider the tastes and personalities of each. When asked about this or that approach to sexual participation in marriage, frequency of intercourse, and the like, the counselor suggests the context of love. Love will lead at least one partner to be sensitive to the other's needs.

Sex is an appetite, like thirst or hunger. Like other appetites, it may be satisfied in various ways, for good or evil. For the best in legitimate sexual gratification, the relationship of love, commitment, fidelity are necessary in the context of a family. There is likelihood that the modern permissive person is, as one analyst stated, "having it more but enjoying it less." The deliberate decision to relate sexual experiences to love and marriage enhances both sex and love. And the Christian is provided biblical guidance for expressing his sexuality in a relationship of love.

God created appetites in man. Without them man would not be motivated. To control those appetites is a Christian's duty. One way of learning control is to relate each appetite to some virtue, such as patience, self-control, moderation, understanding or love. Appetite for food can be controlled by the virtue of moderation. The appetite for sex can be controlled by tender love that generates fidelity and the urge to please one's partner. The Christian should exercise insight that rejects the secular practice that permits man or woman to become animals of gratification. There must be something more than the physical dimension of sex. For the Christian, sex is not merely the manipulation of genitalia. It is a unifying experience providing a mysterious awareness that two have become one.

However, the fact that sexual attraction can be an independent matter from love and marriage should alert men and women to realities that are often masked by romantic idealism. It is likely that any normal human being, man or woman, Christian or non-Christian, even though happily married will be physically attracted to others.

In premarital counseling I ask both the woman and the man how the situation will be handled if one discovers his partner is romantically distracted by another person. The approach of forewarning as forearming has proved helpful in preparing couples for later actual situations. The "offended" mate was able to maintain compassion, firmness, understanding, a prayerful attitude. This has usually been enough to save the marriage. The distracted mate recalled that the problem was discussed before it arose and became reluctant to use rationalizations that are often used to support clandestine relationships. In most cases, the advance knowledge that romantic interest in another is somewhat commonplace, assisted persons in avoiding immorality. The problem was manageable. It is vital that persons remember that sex is not love, but an appetite to be controlled deliberately through love. If sex could not be experienced without love there could be no prostitution.

How Far Have We Come?

It is commonly believed that the problem of sexual adjustment for the younger generation may not be as difficult as it was for their parents. Younger couples are convinced that sexual activity is or ought to be as enjoyable for the wife as for the husband. These couples appear determined to find a mutually satisfying relationship for themselves and to escape the repressive attitudes developed in their parents. To marriage counselors, the new attitude does appear more satisfactory and natural, less selfish, a break with the Victorianism which held sway for a century. Many of the old taboos are dissolved.

However, certain negative results are also appearing. In many cases the new and less repressive attitudes have not translated themselves into commendable action. The divorce rate is high among liberated youth. Selfishness, sexual withdrawal and near animalism (using mates as mere objects for gratification) are more common than the "new freedom" advocates anticipated. Sexual participation seems to be accompanied by less love than formerly, despite the fact that love is dominant in the vocabulary of the young. The result is that there may be nothing left of a relationship after sex.

It is appalling to discover the increase in venereal diseases because of premarital experiences that are defended as appropriate by much of society. The language, habits, attitudes and practices of young men and women, who are supposed to be knowledgeable about themselves, reveal a great deal of ignorance. Unless a better balance is found, the swing from Victorianism to the opposite extreme might create a situation more objectionable than the former repressions.

How to Be a Better Lover

In order to have satisfying sexual activity, both mates in a marriage must have Christian character and understanding. Meeting the needs of others is basic to Christian living and this especially includes meeting the needs of one's mate.

What should be the pattern for husbands? Men need to become better "lovers" (that is to say, use better techniques), better communicators, better planners. They need to develop sensitive, unselfish love. They need to meet each challenge with a gentle aggression that causes them to learn the secret of "a man with a maid." When a sweetheart becomes a wife, she should not cease being the sweetheart. Her husband should continue to win her, to date her, to keep alive the discovery of her. This is vital to the fulfillment of a husband's and wife's sexuality. When he develops this pattern, his wife will not require extensive advice or counsel to understand what is happening or how she should respond.

What should a wife's approach be? When a wife senses the ageless nature of sensuality, that is, that sensuality may be heightened as she grows older, she discovers something of herself she did not know before. Sensuality is in *her*, not in her figure nor even in her sexual organs. It is in her mind, in her attitudes. Her sexuality makes her ageless when it is not unduly sublimated nor flaunted. She should be gentle but aggressive. She should not wait to be conquered, she may give to her husband the same kind of tender loving aggression she desires from him. She should resist the tendency of women to feel that sexual intercourse in some way diminishes her, that she is being unfairly used. She should not interpret the sexual relationship as anything less than the physical completion of the spiritual truth, "the twain shall become one flesh."

Notes

1. *The Seattle Times*, July 18, 1976, p. B9.
2. *Psychology Today*, September 1975, p. 80.
3. Charles McCabe, "Himself," *San Francisco Chronicle*, September 22, 1975, p. 31.
4. Ragan Report, October 27, 1975.
5. *San Francisco Sunday Examiner*, May 9, 1976, p. 4 (Scene).

PART FOUR

MUTUALITY

Greet Priscilla and Aquila my helpers in Christ Jesus: who have for my life laid down their own necks. (Rom. 16:3, 4)

CHAPTER EIGHT

DISCOVERING DIFFERENCES MAKE A DIFFERENCE

Key points in this chapter include:
- what marriage stereotypes are
- what an original marriage is
- how a couple finds mutuality
- how to fill your life space
- how perception relates to mutuality

Who is a wise man and endued with knowledge among you? let him shew out of a good conversation his works with meekness of wisdom. But if ye have bitter envying and strife in your hearts, glory not, and lie not against the truth. This wisdom descendeth not from above, but is earthly, sensual, devilish. For where envying and strife is, there is confusion and every evil work. But the wisdom that is from above is first pure, then peaceable, gentle, and easy to be entreated, full of mercy and good fruits, without partiality, and without hypocrisy. And the fruit of righteousness is sown in peace of them that make peace. (Jas. 3:13-18)

While happiness cannot be guaranteed by calculating the number of mutual interests held by two persons in a relationship, there are compatibility patterns that offer encouragement to a man and woman contemplating life together. Couples occasionally find fulfillment and satisfaction despite their differences, but preponderant evidence proves that marriage is a poor risk for persons who differ widely in interests.

My own marriage is one of the happy exceptions to that general rule. My wife was taken with melancholia during much of her maiden life, and it carried over into extended periods after marriage. During the early years of our relationship this depressive tendency was strong. She was gentle and sensitive, but lacked confidence and was unenergetic. She found it difficult, as she said, to "keep up" with my interests. I was enthusiastic, enjoyed athletics, always busy at my work and aggressive. Friends and enemies thought I sometimes oversimplified problems, but I would forge ahead if I felt that the purpose was worthy of the effort. I loved the night and enjoyed working late hours. I still do.

If my wife and I had not shared a mutual faith, tensions created by our different life-styles and interests might have destroyed our marriage. The agency that held us together until we adjusted to one another was our faith in Christ. That motivation turned us, at last, toward one another rather than away. We desired to do what Christ would have us do in any situation. So in achieving solutions to our problems related to a lack of mutuality, He was present to give us guidance and motivation to change.

Marriage Stereotypes

Marriage tensions are often generated because of dominating stereotypes in cultures. Women sometimes are perceived as housekeepers and mothers, and nothing else. Children are supposed to be "seen and not heard." Father is the wage earner away from home. These are common stereotypes. But many marriages reproduce few of the assumed stereotypes. After observing marriages for years, I am impressed that each couple is special. No counselor has seen, nor may he expect to see, every combination of problems. And new kinds of problems are emerging all the time. Consequently, prescriptive answers appear weak. The various eras change approaches to marriage, as they do to all institutions. Nevertheless, common conceptions and misconceptions of former generations persist, sometimes blocking couples and counselors from discovering solutions.

Persons wrestle with their own confusion about roles in marriage. They try to combine a nineteenth-century conception of a wife and an adjusted twentieth-century conception of a husband. During the nineteenth century most couples lived in a rural or semi-rural environment. Both mother and father were home, or near home, day and night. Father may have been in his field, or in his store at the front of his property, but he was available. Children dealt with father nearly as often as they did with mother. Members of the family labored together to sustain the unit. Women worked as hard and as long as their men, especially when they were farmers, and money earned on the farm or in a small business could have been as fully credited to them as to their husbands. Few labor-saving devices were available for either chores or housekeeping.

Society changed as technology flourished. The most immediate effect was to remove father. He began to work for wages in a location away from the house in which he lived. He saw his wife and children less; he saw other people more.

At first, women continued to live in the former style. Tradition played a part, and women tended to accept the role as guardian of family solidarity. They were encouraged in this role by moral teachers who commended them as God's means for maintaining family continuity for children. The major argument for binding women to their homes was the care of children. Even with the erosion of domestic patterns for women caused by employment opportunities, largely introduced by the needs of a nation in world warfare, the feeling remained strong that the "proper place" of the woman was in the home.

During the last half of the twentieth century many women revolted and insisted on developing a life-style for themselves more free and independent than they had known. As a result a new pattern for family development is emerging. Certainly, there will be serious repercussions for the family especially relating to children.

But if (and that is a large "if") a solution other than continuous mother-care may be found for the needs of young children, there should be no major objection to a woman having the option of choosing both career and marriage. Certainly she should not be forced to be homebound when her children are being satisfactorily cared for or have left the nest. If business houses would inaugurate part-time employment opportunities in half shifts, running say from 9:30 A.M. to 2:00 P.M., many women might find greater fulfillment for themselves even while rearing their small children. This employment policy ought to be a firm and developed plan publicized as standard labor practice throughout the nation. Several companies have experimented with the idea with success.

Every Marriage an Original

Family life stereotypes continue to plague us. In general, stereotypes should be resisted. They shackle persons. False virtue is attached to commonly held ideas based on prejudices. They are the product of revered but oversimplistic patterns and concepts. Seldom are they useful. Some are humorous. Some are shallow. Most persons tend to agree on what the dominant wife stereotype is like. She henpecks her husband with voice, gesture, attitude and demands. But who can be sure of what "henpecking" really is? One assumes he knows when he observes the practice in others. Even this may be illusory. The following experience suggests the stereotyping of a wife who is presumed to henpeck her husband.

In Seattle one spring day I was driving a car full of collegians. They were debaters and I was their coach. We were in the city to compete in a tourney. Next to me sat a young woman student, the wife of the man sitting to her right. The students fell into an animated conversation resulting from an undiplomatic remark made by a young man in the back seat. In referring to the new husband in front, whom we will name Jack, he said, "I think you are henpecked, Jack." His wife, whom we will name Jill, said, icily, "I don't henpeck." Jack defended his wife, and a fervent uncoached debate followed.

I seldom enter a student conversation unless invited. I drove on in silence, until Jack asked me in frustration, "Coach, do you think I am henpecked?"

I replied with a question, as I usually do: "Do you believe you are henpecked?"

"No, I don't," he answered emphatically.

"Then you are not," I said.

This did not satisfy the students. They thought I was evading the issue. They pressed me to elaborate on my answer. I explained that the stereotype of a henpecking woman is based on a person's response to a set of attitudes in the general culture. If neither wife nor husband accepted the stereotype application to their relationship, then observers had misconstrued their experience and the couple was on strong ground. If man and wife were happy and fulfilled with a pattern of conduct that fit them, as long as there were no questions of morality, that conduct was appropriate for them.

Jack then challenged my sophistication when he asked, "But, Coach, do *you* believe I am henpecked?"

I felt that he wanted me to drop my professional mask and define my own subjective feeling, so I said, "Jack, I meant what I said. I do not believe you are henpecked. However, it is my opinion that if I were married to your wife and she talked to me as she does to you, I would believe myself to be henpecked."

But I was not married to the young woman; he was. She and Jack were happy with their marriage pattern. Since that time, they have made a fine marriage, have initiated a growing family and have become professional leaders. I continue to believe my first response, that Jack was not henpecked. He found himself at ease responding to the interests and suggestions of his wife. She was at that time more dynamic and energetic in developing life activities than he was. Later he assumed initiative for some of the couple's new interests. They developed mutuality.

Each husband and wife have the right to create an original family life pattern. There is no biblical injunction for or against fishing, skydiving, golfing, parlor games or rocking in rocking chairs. There is no divine rule that both persons in a marriage must like the same things with similar intensity. However, prospective mates ought to consider that unless there are some similarities in their interests (some mutuality) the chances will be low for happiness in their marriage. The concern in this chapter is for those who feel tension in their relationships because of diversity in interests.

Discovering Mutuality

I often illustrate the differences in likes and dislikes between mates through a simple game. The method is not scientific, but is helpful. I ask audiences of couples to answer a series of questions. The answers are registered by having each member hold up from one to five fingers, showing how strongly he or she feels about a given subject. One finger means "almost no interest"; two fingers, "little interest"; three fingers, "medium interest"; four fingers, "much interest"; five fingers, "near total interest."

The game begins simply with two or three innocuous questions, such as: "How interested are you in this conference?" I ask listeners to hold up their hands, showing one to five fingers. (In this way I ascertain audience understanding of the game.) "How many husbands and wives had at least a one-finger difference with their mates?" (Show of hands.) "How many had a two-finger difference?" (Show of hands.)

I explain the likely meaning of the voting differences between the mates. The larger the difference, the greater the potential problem. One-finger differences may indicate possible sources of difficulty. Two fingers may reveal marked differences. Depending on the importance of the questions asked, a three-finger differential may suggest serious strain between mates on the issue at hand. As a rule, I don't take seriously responses under the three-finger differential. As the game proceeds to more substantial questions, each person reveals his vote only to his mate and together they are to score themselves.

Following public presentation, I have opportunity to counsel husbands and wives who are hostile to each other. They sometimes request private sessions. I have discovered that troubled couples have had one- to four-finger differentials on nearly all vital issues during the question period. The greater the difference in the number of fingers, the greater the hostility appeared to be. Happy wives and husbands tend to vote closely with their mates. Even though on isolated questions there might be clear differences, these are tolerable when large mutuality is present.

Some of the questions I ask are: How interested are you in the church? In your occupation? In your mate's occupation? In the rearing of children? In a vacation? In sports? In sleeping? In hobbies? In clothes? In your home? In spending money? In saving money? In education? In sex? In buying a house? In your marriage? If time permits, the questions may become more specific: How interested are you in television? In making new friends? In the Bible? In talking to your children? In disciplining the children? In saving a specific amount or percentage out of each paycheck? In tithing? In reading books? In talking to each other? In gardening? In going out to dinner? In visiting your in-laws? In listening to Beethoven? In housework? In staying up late?

The primary purpose in the game is to discover mutuality. How close are husband and wife in a large number of interests? If *both* are disinterested in a project that fact is taken as a positive response, just as both sharing the same interest is a positive response. It is at the points of disagreement that tensions arise.

Filling Our Life-Space

A person's life-space is filled by the total of all his activities. The life-space of one person differs from the life-space of another. For example, a wife may devote a large amount of her life-space to her home and children, whereas her husband may designate a smaller amount of his life-space to those areas. A husband may reserve a large percentage of his life-space for his job and hobbies, whereas his wife may have little interest in either and resists any suggestion that she invest time in them. A man who perceives that his job is a very large part of his life-space may, in fact, be putting his occupation ahead of his family. When this occurs, family tension commonly arises.

A particular wife may regard any time given by her husband to his job as excessive. No standard formulas are available to calculate the hours, the concentration and the commitment one should devote to his life's work. One wife complains her husband works too much, another that hers works too little. Both husbands may be working the same number of hours.

Differences in a husband's and a wife's perception of

the prominence of outside work in his or her life-space will have much to do with the happiness of the couple, and with occupational success as well. Communication between partners can easily break down when each attaches great importance to his own use of his life-space as ideal and denigrates any other division of personal time.

Mutual respect may overcome differences in interest. A happy marriage is partially dependent upon the perception each partner has of the other one as a successful person. If a wife perceives her husband to be successful in his career, she is likely to be happy in her marriage and to perform her duties as a wife with enthusiasm. She will be responsive to her successful husband in intimacy, conversation and housekeeping. If she perceives her husband to be a failure, she will reduce her performance in the relationship. Husbands respond in much the same way. If a husband perceives his wife as successful in her roles, he will be more responsive to her in most family categories. We know that unhappy husbands often accuse their wives of poor housekeeping. When she improves, he is happier and she often credits him with improved attitudes. He may have changed very little; she changed significantly.

Mutuality then depends upon several factors: similarities, respect, attitudes, acceptance and perception. In order to develop the ideal in mutuality, creative Christian mates will strive to like and share many of the same interests; they will regard the person and abilities of each other; they will be flexible and sympathetic about the wishes of both; they will resist the temptation to make each other over into some other person; and they will permit a fair amount of individualism to express itself in the marriage partnership.

No couple fully measures up to the ideal but that is

not important if the couple finds ways to "feel" mutuality even when mutuality is not present. A wife who refuses to be irritated by her husband's football interests will feel greater mutuality than one who is irritated and nags her husband about it. A husband who refuses to be irritated by his wife's creation of a thousand macrame hangings will feel greater mutuality than one who is aggravated and grouses about the matter.

Mutuality is helpful to a marriage. It encourages the members to find happiness. But generous persons can adapt themselves and, by strength of good will, maintain their marriages even in the face of differences.

CHAPTER NINE

ACCEPTANCE SOLVES PROBLEMS

Key points in this chapter include:
- when differences in interests can strengthen marriage
- how to resolve educational differences
- how to develop mutuality
- who is expected to change

After these things Paul departed from Athens, and came to Corinth; and found a certain Jew named Aquila, born in Pontus, lately come from Italy, with his wife Priscilla; (because that Claudius had commanded all Jews to depart from Rome:) and came unto them. And because he was of the same craft, he abode with them, and wrought: (for by their occupation they were tentmakers.) ... And he continued there a year and six months, teaching the word of God among them. ... And Paul after this tarried there yet a good while, and then took his leave of the brethren, and sailed thence into Syria, and with him Priscilla and Aquila; having shorn his head in Cenchrea: for he had a vow. And he came to Ephesus, and left them there ... And a certain Jew named Apollos, born at Alexandria, an eloquent man, and mighty in the Scriptures, came to Ephesus. This man was instructed in the way of the Lord; and being fervent in the spirit, he spake and taught diligently the things of the Lord, knowing only the baptism of John. And he began to speak boldly in the synagogue: whom when Aquila and Priscilla had heard, they took him unto them, and expounded unto him the way of God more perfectly. (Acts 18:1-3,11,18, 19,24-26)

The biblical narrative about the marriage of Aquila and Priscilla is tantalizingly sparse. What is known of this husband and wife is highly complimentary to them. They appear to have been inseparable; the activity of one was the activity of the other. As far as we know, they enjoyed total mutuality. When they show up in the narrative, their names appear together as tentmakers, as counselors and evangelists for Apollos, as senders and receivers of church greetings. Their story stretches through a significant period in the ministry of the apostle Paul, beginning at Corinth. There is no record that they had children. They appear to have been as mobile as Paul or any other Christian workers in the first century A.D.

The allusion of the scattered biblical remarks, and from the lack of information, is that Aquila and Priscilla were supportive of each other, were exemplary in their conduct and dedication. Persons knowledgeable of the New Testament are not likely to think of either Aquila or Priscilla separate from the other. Their names imply the highest level of mutuality in marriage. We cannot presume that their success did not require effort, perhaps large effort. They may have shared interests at the time of their wedding, but if they followed common experience they had to work at their purposes. And so do we.

Couples may put together surprising combinations of interests. Sometimes they are successful; sometimes they are not. A few short summaries of case histories may show the opportunities for creative solutions, as well as some of the pitfalls.

A husband was interested in sports and his wife in music. This couple solved the problem by following their separate interests independently but at the same time. This allowed them time to pursue other mutual interests together. The wife's best practice sessions took place while he rooted for his team in the stadium or in the television room. The piano was quite removed from the TV room.

In this case maturity, mutual acceptance, and trade-off between husband and wife minimized conflict. These should be standard practices and attitudes with all couples, but they are not. This particular couple, early in marriage, learned how to solve their problem by mutual tolerance and generosity. Their experience provided practicable approaches for solving other conflicts later. They followed a plan in their problem-solving. Each traded off a pleasant result to the other in order to gain support for an interest he himself wanted to pursue.

A second couple did not fare as well. The husband fancied himself sufficiently skilled to become a golf professional. His "golf widow" chafed and complained about the pattern and schedule of their lives. The man was a happy and easygoing fellow, but he was insensitive to her problems. He had virtually made golf his mistress. Only his untimely death prevented the collapse of the marriage in divorce. The woman's second marriage was to a different sort of man.

In another couple the woman was interested in books and her husband in "nothing." This one failed because of the "nothing." The man was an asocial, apathetic person whose life appeared devoid of flavor or purpose. He was among those individuals who are arrested in their cultural growth.

"Nothing" persons become fugitives from themselves. They appear to have no desire to become involved with life and family members or others. Marriage is threatened when one partner has no interest outside of himself. Even so, some one-sided marriages survive because the energetic partner is adaptable and, perhaps, because the apathetic person has an intense secret admiration for the active mate.

Some marriages die because either husband or wife stops growing intellectually. The failure in intellectual growth by one partner is seldom referred to in divorce proceedings, but it is more of a factor in marriage failure than is commonly believed.

One strange case involved a complete reversal by both partners in their interests. The man was a party lover. His wife resisted. Her upbringing and inclination made her uncomfortable in a boisterous atmosphere. She made her feelings known but joined her husband in attending parties of various kinds. Her attendance seemed the only way she could save her marriage. In time she became more comfortable—she even began to enjoy herself a little.

Then he began to change. The change was imperceptible at first. The crisis came when he observed a man make a gesture of affection toward his wife. He began to withdraw from partying, but he discovered that his wife had become very interested in that life-style. She was titillated by attention from other men. She had cultivated an enjoyment for the activities and participation she had earlier deplored. The marriage collapsed and was ended.

Another man was interested in a lodge, and his wife in a church. But the problem was talked out and resolved amicably. The woman was free to follow her spiritual goals and the man limited his fraternal interests somewhat. Neither tried to coerce the other into sharing his or her interests.

Often the church member creates situations that appear judgmental of the nonchurch member. Judgmentalism is always a danger signal in personal relationships. Aside from bearing a clear and penetrating witness about one's faith to his mate, the believer must leave the rest of the action to God's providence. The only remaining duties for the Christian mate are to pray, privately if necessary, and live an exemplary life. The problem of religious aggression that might arise here is discussed in chapter 4.

It Helps to "Grow Up"

Insight about interests may not emerge until after marriage. Young men and women marry when they are still socially and culturally underdeveloped. Subsequently, latent interests may be discovered or new ones developed. This is especially true of persons who wed at younger than average ages for marriage. Many youths have not thought deeply about life's complexities and responsibilities, but will do so as they mature. There may be a considerable difference in the development of one partner over the other during the first 10 or 20 years of marriage.

Some persons never "grow up." At the time of the wedding both partners appear compatible, but later one matures and leaves the other behind. In some cases playgirl types marry playboy types, but in a few years the playboy makes a radical turn and seeks new dimensions for life. In other cases, one mate may be perceptibly more mature than the other but proceeds with the marriage hoping for better things in the future. Bitter disappointment follows when the less mature mate shows no intention of changing or growing. Tension and disappointment are likely to develop in any marriage in which one spouse becomes significantly more mature than the other.

Any marriage may be presumed to possess potential for survival. Something brought the husband and wife together at the beginning. With assistance the family can be saved, if the couple evidences willingness to work out problems. Each person must resist the desire to make over the other in a predetermined image. Both must agree that shifts in conduct require shifts in atti-

134

tudes, and these shifts should be mutually agreed upon.

A veteran counselor senses, during the first two or three sessions with a couple, if there is a will to conciliate. Without that energy, extended counseling will not likely be useful. If there is little agreement in adaptation and no flexibility, a couple will not discover mutuality.

Differences in interests need not destroy a marriage. They may be used creatively to strengthen it. One woman may learn to identify by cultivating personal interest in her husband's hobby, but another may succeed without actual participation.

In one instance the wife knitted while her husband bowled. Her few attempts at the sport beloved by her husband were frustrating. The gutter seemed to draw her ball as a magnet draws metal filings. She could keep score well, enjoy conversation—and knit. Her response to their "problem" made the matter no problem at all. On the contrary, she created a situation that strengthened their relationship. On many occasions they went to the bowling alley with another couple. That wife was also a nonparticipant. The women talked; the men bowled. There were refreshments, some nonsense conversation between couples, and meaningful fellowship. Mates were together and no one was bored. The plan worked well.

A man accepted his wife's interest in music, although he did not really warm to her classical interests, or, for that matter, to music at all. He transported his wife to concerts and recitals, sometimes attended, and tried sincerely to learn to enjoy the programs. He never quite succeeded for himself, but his marriage was sound. He did not believe life had to be exactly as he would have designed it. He recognized his duty to encourage his wife. She did not expect from him total commitment to her interests or ecstasy over music. She readily released him for his interests. Again, maturity and trade-off overcame possible problems.

Educational Differences and Mutuality

The differing speed of growth between partners can be especially troublesome if the couple determines to pursue formal education for one member. Following World War II a significant change in marriage and education patterns took place in American society. Rather than delay marriage until education was completed and the individuals were professionally established, young people married first. The young bride worked for her "PHT" degree, as was said at the time—Putting Hubby Through. While the husband earned an education, the wife tended to remain intellectually stagnant. The care for her husband, her job, their home and perhaps an infant or two occupied her time.

During the years following his graduation, this well-educated professional man may have found his wife to be unsatisfactory intellectually and socially, so the marriage was ended. The husband was willing to accept immediate condemnation and loss of friends in order to construct a new life relationship. Differences in educational achievements created differences in interests. This kind of difference seems to be more important to educated persons than to those who have had less formal education.

One of the tragedies of educational differentials is the inner private suffering of the less-educated partner, usually the wife. She begins to feel inferior to her husband as she notes his progress. Her self-esteem declines: Even if her husband does not misuse his greater sophistication through psychological aggression, she may sense inadequacy in herself. She becomes unhappy, perhaps bitter, with her marriage.

How can a couple resolve problems resulting from different educational levels? At the very least, the less-educated wife should make a special effort to become aware of everything around her, to see and listen and think. She should ask meaningful questions. If she plans carefully her time and involvement, she may become a reader and, to a degree at least, educate herself. If her husband is empathic, he may assist by sharing his knowledge. This will be a delicate matter if either partner is unduly sensitive or exudes an illusion of superiority during exchanges.

Increasingly, communities are providing adult education. Only laziness or the tendency to vegetate keep most men and women from improving their minds. Some individuals are markedly successful in taking advantage of opportunities. One wife determined to follow through on her formal education until she completed a doctoral degree. Her husband concentrated on her achievement. She did not neglect her wifely duties. When she completed her program, she concentrated upon her husband's interests. He responded to encouragement and began his own program of studies. Ultimately, he sold his business and launched a new and exciting career. The conclusion was a happy one.

A second couple discovered that both of them had an emerging interest in education. The husband wished to advance his program but was slower than his wife in completing requirements. Competition might threaten their relationship. In concern for her marriage, the woman slowed her own progress. She ultimately succeeded in nearly all her purposes, and so did her husband.

Resolving Differences in Mutuality

Someone has pointed out that a key to solving troubled relationships may be found in looking at the entries for "give" and "take" in *Webster's Unabridged Dictionary*. There are 66 column-inches devoted to the definitions of "take" and 22 column-inches to "give." The balance is 3 to 1 in favor of the kind of conduct that we consider less desirable. Apparently men and women are more efficient at "taking" than "giving." Without a giving spirit there will be little mutuality in marriage, and without a share of mutuality a couple will not likely find happiness.

Some ways of developing mutuality include trade-off, self-improvement, personal change, self and mate acceptance, and marital counseling. There are other practices that offer hope and promise. Acceptance of what *is* may be a necessary first step for both husband and wife. There are women who learn to accept their husbands as fishermen, hunters, TV enthusiasts, and hobby followers without joining them in those pursuits. Husbands, in turn, come to accept adjustments in the way they divide their time between work, hobbies and family. In most cases, wives have their own interests as well. Some couples are able, by careful programming, to pursue independent professional careers. They may have separate sets of friends and travel apart from one another for professional or recreational purposes. Consequently, they spend very little time together. Yet, generosity of spirit and personal trust enable them to develop a satisfying marriage and keep them faithful to one another. However, very few persons appear able to order their lives in this generous manner.

Considerateness is the key. Not all women object to their husbands' activities in which they have no part. Some wives only ask that their men be thoughtful and aware—include a portion of time for mutual interests or fellowship and maintain communication lines. Wives who complain most about becoming "golf widows" or the like are often neglected in other areas of the marriage as well. They focus their blame on the obvious hobby. They might accept some of their husbands' diversions from mutual interests. But they are suspicious of being overlooked altogether.

Change and Mutuality

Change is inevitable, of course. Resistant attitudes may slow it up. If the differences between two persons become severe, more rapid change is required in at least one member for survival of their marriage. James Bellamy, family counselor, affirmed the inevitability of change between husband and wife:

> Each of us constantly is changing. If we're not growing, we're deteriorating. If we're not improving life, we're drifting. A common problem is that one or the other in a marriage changes at a different rate.[1]

As a general rule, the stronger partner must make the changes, for the weaker is unable or unwilling to do so. In counseling sessions the stronger person often contends that the weaker should submit, and the weaker is assumed to be in error when a conflict arises. The biblical principle holds here: the strong should make greater allowances. Yielding to the "weaker vessel" is a proof of strength. One evidence of weakness is the inability to be flexible. To request change in a weaker partner may be to ask for something that, given the time and circumstances, cannot be granted. A common problem with strong persons is that they expect acquaintances to function at the high level on which they function. But those on whom they impose the standard possess insufficient resources or understanding of themselves to perform on that high level.

139

Adaptation to one another's interests is generally the solution that emerges from counseling sessions. It is the best approach to take if a husband and wife are to move toward each other emotionally, if they are to enjoy their relationship and find fulfillment. When a person is flexible, the mate is permitted to remain himself and generosity grows up between husband and wife. Each adopts at least some of the interests of the other, but he still maintains his own individuality. In later years each will appreciate the other for not robbing him of some special activity that was fulfilling.

Premarital counseling is helpful for understanding potential interest problems. Possible pitfalls may be understood before the marriage. Even where they have not been completely resolved, possible problem areas will be helped with partial awareness and insights that grow out of counseling exchanges. The couple can determine in advance to face up to problems as they arise. Much of the current tension leading to marriage breakup could be significantly reduced if old-fashioned determination could be recaptured. Earlier generations seemed to know that determination was integral to marriage. Imperfection in the partner and in the relationship could be accommodated.

Genuine merging of interests may require several years to accomplish, if "togetherness" is to happen at all. When a couple is able to recall that during premarital counseling, problem areas were identified and options reviewed, the chances for survival of that relationship improve greatly.

It is helpful to remind oneself that no man and woman are fully compatible. Compatibility can be learned, but it remains imperfect. It grows with effort, acceptance, learning and unselfishness. Prospective bride and groom should be made to understand that they *are* incompatible. They should prepare themselves for inevitable differences. They will become compatible only through awareness of their own humanity and the genuine needs of their mates. Each then tries to meet the needs of the other. Wise persons choose their course; the remainder live by a series of accidents.

A *couple*, as a couple, will either change deliberately or by an unguided and imperceptible evolution throughout marriage. The *individual* also changes within his or her changing marriage so that the whole matter becomes complex. An individual may be changing in one direction, let us say, for the good, while the couple is changing in another direction, let us say, for the bad.

Newly married couples may appear to make dramatic changes in their interests. However, these changes are generally superficial and experimental. They may not be truly beneficial. For example, a couple as a unit may be either corrupted or improved by new friends whose lifestyle seems attractive to them. But as values out of their past surface and show energy, the husband and wife may find themselves at odds over the changes which have occurred in them as a couple. A woman joined her husband as a "party girl." In three years her experiences palled. Her personal values surfaced and competed with the interests introduced by her husband. Her reversion back to her former values offended him. Deep unhappiness followed. She had been willing to try these new interests, but she was unwilling to continue in them. The marriage failed.

Changes ought to be based on criteria that promise positive rather than negative change to the family unit. If husband and wife think of themselves as one, they tend to reinforce each other in behavior and values that are acceptable to both. They can generally discover the areas of agreement and capitalize on those.

For instance, a couple may desire a quiet and tranquil home. The husband may be an avid reader and the wife a dressmaker. It is not necessary for both to become readers to gain a sense of unity in their interests. The unity of the couple is not in their separate activities but in their love of quietness and solitude. Working together, at separate interests, in silence, becomes a mutual value for wife and husband. Either could choose any number of distractions in the quiet environment. As long as they preserve the mutual value, a tranquil atmosphere, they may be expected to find happiness.

Mutuality That Lasts

A general principle holds that whatever a couple may share mutually will tend to strengthen their marriage. The principle applies to religious as well as other issues. Perhaps it applies even more fully to religious concerns. For example, if a couple attempts to live according to Scripture, the effort is likely to be easier for both mates than if either attempts to do so. Each reinforces the high priorities of the other. Of course, a great many homes are divided in faith. A person may survive and grow in his spiritual life even if he is alone in his effort. It is, however, more difficult for one alone than for two working at the same purpose.

An important key to resolution to such problems is that both partners should assert, before they begin to work on change, that they are irrevocably committed to each other. They should reject in advance the option to separate or divorce. Commitment to solidarity is a basic element in achieving the solutions hoped for. It forces the couple to look elsewhere than escape for solutions. They force themselves to learn to cope with marital tension.

A man and wife who love Christ ought to be able to

learn to love one another. If that principle does not prove itself in my marriage, either my wife or I—or both of us—have failed. The breakup of marriages in which both husbands and wives affirm that they are devoted Christians poses a significant dilemma. God loves them and they love God. They can, if they will, love each other. The Christian virtues of patience, humility, grace, acceptance and devotion are the large resources from Christ which make living and loving effective. They are large enough to make marriage beautiful even when mutuality is not total. In the end, husband and wife discover that Christian faith afforded the largest of all mutualities—eternity.

Note

1. James Bellamy, *The Seattle Times*, July 18, 1976, p. A7.

PART FIVE

MONEY

Do good, . . . be rich in good works, ready to distribute, willing to communicate. (1 Tim. 6:18)

CHAPTER TEN

MONEY IS
THE MISERY MAKER

Key points in this chapter include:
- why money is important in marriage
- who is most likely to succeed at money management—husband or wife
- why parents are not effective teachers of money management

If any man teach otherwise, and consent not to wholesome words, even the words of our Lord Jesus Christ, and to the doctrine which is according to godliness; he is proud, knowing nothing, but doting about questions and strifes of words, whereof cometh envy, strife, railings, evil surmisings, perverse disputings of men of corrupt minds, and destitute of the truth, supposing that gain is godliness: from such withdraw thyself. But godliness with contentment is great gain. For we brought nothing into this world, and it is certain we can carry nothing out. And having food and raiment, let us be therewith content. But they that will be rich fall into temptation and a snare, and into many foolish and hurtful lusts, which drown men in destruction and perdition. For the love of money is the root of all evil: which while some coveted after, they have erred from the faith, and pierced themselves through with many sorrows. But thou, O man of God, flee these things; and follow after righteousness, godliness, faith, love, patience, meekness. . . . Charge them that are rich in this world, that they be not high-minded, nor trust in uncertain riches, but in the living God, who giveth us richly all things to enjoy; that they do good, that they be rich in good works, ready to distribute, willing to communicate; laying up in store for themselves a good foundation against the time to come, that they may lay hold on eternal life. (1 Tim. 6:3-11,17-19)

The mismanagement of money is generally ranked by

148

analysts as a leading cause of contention in marriage. Lester Velie writes: "What breaks up the young marriages? Lack of sex? Lack of communication? Lack of freedom? A lack of something in the marriage itself? Nonsense. It is lack of money. Or, to put it another way, lack of preparation for the job of supporting a family."[1] In his popular column, L.M. Boyd asserts: "Lack of money is the number one reason why men run away from their wives, according to a professional fellow who makes a living trying to find straying husbands. He contends there is nothing so likely to send a husband on his lonely way as the guilty notion he can't come up with a livelihood. Nagging is reason number two."[2] Joyce Brothers succinctly summarizes the issue: "Disputes about money and how it is to be spent send more couples to marriage counselors than all other causes combined."[3]

McCall's magazine took a poll of its readers and discovered that women were most discontented in marriage with housework. Second to this they mentioned finances. Asked what caused most arguments, the largest group of respondents (30 percent) named money. Other subjects for quarrels included, in descending order: children, friends, relatives, leisure time, habits and personal appearance. Only a small percentage referred to sex.[4] When all the evidence is reviewed, it is clear that money management is a major problem area in marriage, possibly the number one troublemaker.

Conflict about money is an issue in Christian as well as non-Christian marriages. In marriages where one or both partners is an evangelical, there are some unique aspects of the problem. For example, giving to Christian causes sometimes creates tension in a family divided by differences in religious dedication. Tithing may be a tense issue even in a Christian family where husband

and wife are both committed Christians. The mates view stewardship duties unevenly. Unchurched families may not think about giving money away on a regular schedule at a predetermined rate, so the question of charitable donations is not likely to cause family strife. On the other hand, Christian couples are not likely to encounter as much difficulty as non-Christians on expenditures for entertainment. Liquor bills alone cause unending debate in many homes.

However, except for significant exceptions, the economic problems encountered by Christian and non-Christian families are similar. Balancing checkbooks, avoiding credit card excesses, and general overspending are common issues. Christian families appear to manage their incomes with better-than-average skill. The uses to which money is put by Christians is closely related to their values and sense of stewardship.

Why Money Is Important in Marriage

Money is an important means by which persons influence or manipulate others. There is an aura of authority about money because it is an effective motivational factor, and the highest tangible reward for work. It can be traded for nearly anything in the material world. It is easily calculated and conveniently handled as a standard value system for business.

Most persons understand this significance of money. They know that virtually all physical human needs may be met by an adequate supply of money. A man labors in the hope that he will make as much income as possible so that he may achieve specified purposes. These goals usually cannot be accomplished without money. Or he may wish to accumulate wealth for the purpose of being remembered after death for the bequests he leaves. He may not be able to take his money with him, but he can leave behind some evidence that he was here. In life or in death one achieves status with money.

Most members of a family believe that the person earning the money for a household wields greatest power in the family. Traditionally there has been a consistent relationship between the supplier of money and ultimate authority in the family. This pattern may change in the future. Counselors are discovering among younger people a declining accent on connection between economic power and authority. This is in part due to the philosophy of the youth movement, which has lowered the respect for labor and affluence. There are advantages and disadvantages in the new style. Reduction of authority weakens one of the breadwinner's motives for hard work. Jobs in an industrial society are commonly repetitive, sometimes dehumanizing. Laborers often complain about job monotony. Unhappiness with their work is deep.[5]

Menial work has never been overly popular, but it has been generally accepted as the only practical means for providing family needs in a technological society. Taking away the honor of family authority afforded to the wage earner may make labor even less attractive. It removes one of his primary motivations for work. Society may encounter difficulty in declining productivity arising from such reduced motivation. There are evidences that the decline has begun in the western world and that it affects family patterns and solidarity.

The connection between money and authority is seen not only in the family, but in society at large. The general rule has been that the higher the status that is attributed to an office, the greater should be the salary and authority connected with it. Or, the larger the responsibility is presumed to be, the larger should be the income for carrying it. As authority figures gain in affluence, their money increases their power and influence. Persons of wealth generally receive deference from those around them and their ideas are respected more highly than those of poor men.

This status through wealth is illustrated in a research project which utilized the services of a "jaywalker." It was discovered that a well-dressed, prosperous looking man motivated others to break local traffic laws by walking across a street against a red stoplight. His conduct stimulated men and women, strangers to him, standing on the same corner, to follow him against the light. They were persuaded by his appearance of affluence. They subconsciously believed in him as a responsible person. Later, when the same man was dressed as a poor and somewhat bedraggled derelict, his lawbreaking was met with hard stares and murmurings. Pedestrians near him did not follow his lead as they had before. They felt: "People like that have no respect for the law." Other research verifies the fact that persons perceived to be affluent are given greater authority by people around them than those perceived to be poor.

Differing Attitudes Cause Tension

It is common for husband and wife to have different attitudes relative to money. Both tend to be defensive of their viewpoints about family funds. As a rule women are more frugal in spending than men. They tend to give away less until personal security is guaranteed, tip less, and buy fewer luxuries than their husbands. However, Christian women are at least as generous as their husbands in giving to the church. If limited income is available and a tight budget must be kept, a woman is more likely to succeed at family money management than a man. One poll showed that 57 percent of the families queried managed their funds through primary control by the wife, 24 percent were managed by the husband, and 19 percent were directed by husband and wife in a team effort. Each group recorded both success and failure, but wives appeared to hold the edge for success in money management.

Despite the fact that most wives are more frugal than their husbands, there are many exceptions to the generality. One woman humorously stated in counseling sessions: "I have nearly ruined our marriage with my spending. When it comes to credit cards, I have the fastest draw in the West." When a wife does become a spendthrift, she seems to shop and buy without reason. By such conduct she may be calling for help in some other matter as many arsonists and thieves appear to be calling out for assistance with their personal problems. Any extremes of miserliness or spending may be symptoms of problems unrelated to money.

The Breadwinner/Autocrat

Because possession or control of money represents significant authority, a family must be protected from undue autocracy by the family breadwinner. This protection is afforded through love in the family, through advance budget agreements, through faithful communication, through appropriate reduction in the value placed on money, and through recognition that the roles of individual members of a family are equally important. Some member or members of a family must take on the roles of wage earner or earners. The roles taken by other family members are not, or should not be, unduly subject to control by the moneymaker.

A woman must bear a child if one is to be born. In this way she fulfills her physical role. Thus far society has not put a price tag on the bearing of a child, but all would agree that it is a necessary contribution to the family.

Mother and infant should not become victims of a husband and father simply because his contribution to the family is monetary while theirs is not. A woman's role of mother and housewife effectively performed (if she chooses not to follow an occupational career) should be recognized as proof of her investment in the family, to be matched by proof of her husband's commitment through breadwinning. The reward of her effort is her child and her well-ordered home. His reward is awareness that he is an adequate provider. All must be appreciated for their contributions. In these roles both husband and wife are partially fulfilled. The rewards should be amicably shared. A marriage is happier when authority is based on higher criteria than moneymaking ability. And happier still when both spouses avoid the "this is mine and that is yours" syndrome.

Open communication is vital in easing tensions about spending. The one who chiefly handles the payout should not be offended at any question about finances by the mate. ("What did this check pay for?" or, "I thought we paid for that last month.") And the answers to the questions should be factual and positive. (Not, "What's the matter, don't you trust me?" but, "That check was for a gift to the newlyweds," or, "I meant to pay it last month but forgot until we were billed again.") The tone of the question and the tone of the answer are keys to communication effectiveness.

Sven Wahlroos affirmed the difference between negative and positive communication in budget matters:

Wife: "Do you think we can afford a new refrigerator?"

Negative husband: "There you go again with your constant demands."

Positive husband: "Let's go over the budget together and see."[6]

Money Means Security

Family disagreements arise over money because money or its absence represents much of what the family may or may not do. Sufficient money assures a family that they can purchase the things they need to sustain them and gain some of the members' life goals. These may include security in old age, mobility and freedom, symbols of success, a sense of well-being, care of one's family, and an awareness that worthy institutions or persons may be assisted through personal stewardship.

Tension sometimes arises in a marriage over how much money is earned—the wage or salary level. The husband gains a reputation with his wife as a "good" or "poor" provider. If she sees him as a "poor" provider, she tends to lose respect for him. If she sees him as a "good" provider, she tends to acknowledge his prowess to others, for her own worth is partly evaluated in the manner of man she attracts and marries.

At the outset of marriage money problems may be acute. Needs commonly are greater, or seem so, in young families than old. Men and women who marry leave their parental homes after the family has already greatly reduced financial tensions. They are unaware of, or forget, the difficult years their parents encountered. A young husband's small wage seems unsatisfactory compared to the larger one his wife remembers from her father's home. Resources are low and needs great at the beginning, especially after the birth of a child. And the society is not set up to provide fully for the needs and wants of young families.

On the other hand, young marrieds who begin with high bank balances and are not faced with the effort to make ends meet are not exempt from financial conflicts. Available evidence suggests that affluent young couples have babies later than their less prosperous friends. They are also less likely to donate significantly to church or charity. They tend to accent selfish interests. Their conflicts over money are generally severe and focus on differences of interests and values. Early marriage is for them, as for those struggling financially, a time of tension and adjustment to one another. They do not appear to hold advantage over their less affluent young friends.

Parental Programming About Money

Those contemplating matrimony do not generally think through the importance of money or living standards in a new marriage. Life-styles developed from a childhood of poverty in the case of one mate and wealth for the other may pose problems that cause tension for newlyweds.

A woman, married and divorced twice, recited her distress several times over a long period of counseling. She could not hold either of her husbands, but could not understand why. She could not see that most men in whom she would be interested would not tolerate her casual housekeeping.

I argued for better order in her habits and her home. She clearly illustrated my point when she turned the subject suddenly to my home, saying: "I could not live in a house that is as clean as yours. For me, there must be papers and clothes strewn around. Your house makes me uncomfortable. My husband can't stay home because he is neat. I have always been sloppy. I was brought up that way. We were poor and no one cared about the place. Why do I always become involved with neat people?"

The woman was programmed in her parental home to be casual, even sloppy, and was unable to handle the life-style of relative affluence. She will probably live all her life on some form of public assistance. Although her welfare payments were low, she managed well. She paid her rent and bought what her children needed. She made regular contributions to the church. She was not in debt. The real damage was to her person. She had not developed a sense of self-reliance. She seemed doomed to live her life as a lonely, wistful woman.

Parents are about as effective as teachers of money management as they are of sex information. Both subjects are usually handled poorly. A family's economic performance makes such an impact on the children of that family that money-handling problems in their own future marriages are conditioned by it. Miserly parents do not rear children capable of healthy financial planning. Neither do spendthrifts. Parents who are penurious or big spenders are poor examples of money management for their children. Family goals, family values, and a basic understanding of what money is and does are vital to teaching children how to handle business affairs.

Only in this century have most families needed to be occupied with budget planning. Their forefathers were fortunate if they were able to save a little for retirement. Most were dependent upon their grown children, who, by carrying responsibility for the aged, earned their inheritance. And persons did not live as long as they do today. Average longevity in 1776 was under 36 years: in 1976, nearly 72 years, or double the 1776 figure. The largest gain has been since 1900. There were six persons in the average 1776 American family: in 1976 the average was less than three and a half. For the general populace in 1776 not a great deal of money exchange took place. There was a great emphasis on thrift with the little currency available. Benjamin Franklin's aphorism, "A penny saved is a penny earned," was afforded nearly the authority of Holy Writ.

In the current century, increased cash flow and the decline of farm life with its semi-barter system have required a new emphasis on family management of funds. A family may handle more money during the years of its life than a small business would have handled in the same period of time in the nineteenth century. Each year an average family takes in, spends and pays taxes in larger amounts than could have been imagined a century ago. Income taxes were unknown in the United States until 1912. Many families in the United States and Canada handle a half-million to a million dollars during the lifetime of a single wage earner. And they are never presumed to be rich. Most wage earners leave only modest estates, many nothing at all, after managing the equivalent of a fortune during a lifetime.

The new skill of family money management should be taught to students in high school. There is a growing body of literature on the subject. A new phenomenon occurred during the period following World War I— average men and women became meaningful shareholders in the national wealth. They bought stocks and bonds, often on speculation. But they were not well prepared to manage their share in the national wealth. The great depression caught them by surprise. The American public learned some lessons from that experience, but their spending patterns suggest that they have not yet learned how to handle finances skillfully.

The modern family encounters money problems from the outset. Even the honeymoon may put the bride and groom in debt. The couple immediately faces house and transportation costs. Education loans may hang heavily over them. Necessities must be purchased.

With little school or home education to guide the

couple, the future may appear to be threatening. But with patience, prudence, and control a family budget can be designed and followed. There is a kind of euphoria that occurs in persons who are solvent. If they are able to save a portion of their income, the animation is further heightened. And when there has been sufficient practice in effective money management, the couple will enjoy the good feeling and reject the enslavement of debt. Large debt erodes freedom. Prudence and control in fiscal matters releases energy in a family for other purposes, for growth and personal investment.

Notes

1. Lester Velie, "The Myth of the Vanishing Family," *Readers Digest* (February, 1973), p. 113.
2. *San Francisco Chronicle*, June 2, 1973, p. 33.
3. *San Francisco Examiner*, August 19, 1973.
4. *San Francisco Examiner*, May 9, 1976.
5. Studs Terkel, *Working* (New York: Pantheon, 1974), p. 1ff.
6. Sven Wahlroos, *Family Communication* (New York: Macmillan, 1974), p. 26.

CHAPTER ELEVEN

PLANNING POINTS THE WAY TO HAPPINESS

Key points in this chapter include:
- how to calculate all income as family property
- why Christians should be prosperous
- what the 10-80-10 plan can do
- how warning signals indicate poor fiscal planning
- how to find the joys of a debt-free existence

Now therefore perform the doing of it; that as there was a readiness to will, so there may be a performance also out of that which ye have. For if there be first a willing mind, it is accepted according to that a man hath, and not according to that he hath not. For I mean not that other men be eased, and ye burdened: But by an equality, that now at this time your abundance may be a supply for their want, that their abundance also may be a supply for your want; that there may be equality: As it is written, He that hath gathered much had nothing over; and he that had gathered little had no lack. . . .

Therefore I thought it necessary to exhort the brethren, that they would go before unto you, and make up beforehand your bounty, whereof ye had notice before, that the same might be ready, as a matter of bounty, and not as of covetousness. But this I say, He which soweth sparingly shall reap also sparingly; and he which soweth bountifully shall reap also bountifully. Every man according as he purposeth in his heart, so let him give; not grudgingly, or of necessity: for God loveth a cheerful giver. And God is able to make all grace abound toward you; that ye, always having all sufficiency in all things, may abound to every good work. (2 Cor. 8:11-15; 9:5-8)

While handling money is a problem for many marriages, good financial management is no real mystery. It takes teamwork, discipline and readiness for communication between husband and wife.

If husband and wife work, both should contribute their earnings to the family coffers. As a general rule, all income of both persons should be placed in a mutual treasury. In some cases a man and woman are independently wealthy and agree on a division of their property before marriage. But in most cases separation of accounts is not conducive to trust and the building of unity. The biblical pattern is that husband and wife should be united in every way possible. The two have been made one flesh. To divide funds is to operate in a way that goes against the basic ideal of unity in marriage. Combining earnings and accounts does not eliminate the possibility of developing special allowances and projects or personal bank accounts by mutual consent. In any event, if the couple is responsible in stewardship, happy and solvent, any system they amicably choose to follow is satisfactory.

One generally detects some disillusionment in a marriage that attaches "his" and "hers" to money earned or inherited, or to other property. But there are some circumstances in which division is advisable. For example, some couples learn to live on his income and save hers. Accounts are separated to guarantee compliance with the plan. This procedure develops discipline, permits the family to pursue special goals and allows flexibility for the family. However, the money saved should be "ours" rather than "his" or "hers." Eventually, the couple will use their savings for family purposes, such as the formal education of children, or travel, or retirement.

Should Christians Be Prosperous?

A couple should strive for financial success and security. In the Christian community there appears to be considerable misunderstanding about success as it relates to the use and accumulation of money. Some hypocrisy is evident, for though poverty and self-denial are exalted as the ideal for Christians, those who have obvious success and wealth are shown special deference. Many Christians seem proud that some of their own have "made it." Those affluent believers have encountered the world of competition, preserved their Christian integrity, and succeeded.

The Bible, notably the Old Testament, attaches high value to prosperity. And prosperity was valued because it was evidence of God's favor for His people. Job's personal prosperity was assumed to be a sign of God's blessing. When his health and wealth were gone, he was accused of failing God. His restoration to wealth was interpreted as God's doing. When Solomon became king, his prosperity related to God's blessing. When kings abandoned God the economy declined. Archaeologists sometimes refer to the differences in artifacts as representative of the shifting wealth/faith and poverty/unfaith cycles of ancient Israel. Abijah said to Israel, "Fight ye not against the Lord God of your fathers; for ye shall not prosper" (2 Chron. 13:12). And the psalmist stated that the paths of God "drop fatness" (Ps. 65:11). The poet had not seen God's people "begging bread" because God was "ever merciful" (Ps. 37: 25,26).

The crux of the matter is that God provides the prosperity. It is not the result of human cleverness or sheer talent but God's control in one's life—in occupation, money, purposes, judgment, and priorities. This affirmation does not deny the importance of skill. Skill is often one of the tools through which God works and by which He may make a family prosperous. Many competent Christian men and women affirm that God runs their business. They often dedicate resultant profits to advance the Kingdom of God on earth.

Money Reveals Values

A value system may be extracted from the way a person or family spends money. If a family saves money, gives to worthy causes, buys necessities, shuns debt, it is possible for an analyst to project what its values are, not only in the matter of money but in other areas as well. If family members incur heavy debts, do not save, and, because of financial pressure, feel they cannot give to church or charity, the value system is obviously different from that of the first family. Some persons never have enough money. They become insatiable in their appetite for it. They fall in love with money. Their values are distorted, for money accumulation becomes an end in itself.

The Scriptures affirm: "The love of money is the root of all evil." The important clarification here is that it is the "love" of money which is the culprit rather than money itself. It is significant that Jesus came into contact with many wealthy persons. He did not focus on their wealth but on their attitude toward their riches. In many instances He accepted the hospitality of affluent persons. Their wealth seems not to have been a problem to Jesus until it negatively affected life purposes.

Christians are not exempt from the temptation to live for material gain alone. Greed is a common and tenacious evil. The desire to accumulate wealth for its own sake must sometimes be overcome by the most devout persons. Miserly conduct seems uglier in Christians than in others. Jesus warned of this danger and illustrated His point in the story of the man who would build new and larger barns to accommodate a bumper crop. To buy and sell and get gain became this man's whole purpose. His soul was required of him the very day he made the decision to commit himself to this purpose and he was called a fool. Jesus also talked to a rich young ruler whose only evil was the love of his wealth. But this attitude, as far as we know, prevented his salvation.

Solutions to money problems should be based on ideals governing family finances. One ideal ought to be efficiency. Who should manage the family funds? That person who can do the best job of it. Nowhere does Scripture teach that one partner or the other should manage family funds. The wise couple will assign the best manager in the home to function as the bookkeeper or treasurer. A man does not give up his manhood or his role in the family when his wife balances accounts. In this, as in other matters, attitudes of the family members determine which solution is best. Businesses are run by presidents and managers, not bookkeepers and treasurers. Corporate presidents might make poor treasurers, and vice versa. Family money management is analogous. Those with talents for financial matters ought to use them with encouragement from other family members.

The 10-80-10 Plan

Regardless of who actually maintains family records, both mates have a right to information about financial affairs and both should have a voice in what is done with money. This involvement is initiated by agreeing on a budget. I believe the best family budget is one built around the 10-80-10 plan. No family may be said to have a satisfactory approach to their use of money if they do not give away a portion of their income and save another portion. The 10-80-10 plan assumes that each family should live on 80 percent of its income and divide the other 20 percent between savings and donations.

Double "tithe" of an income, reserving half for personal savings and half for church donations, satisfies human needs to share and to build security.

In premarital counseling sessions the 10-80-10 principle has proved very helpful. Even students working their way through college and marrying before completing their educational course find the plan effective. No complaint has ever returned to me that it had been tried and could not be done. Most couples, at the time of counseling, said that they thought they could not save until they were well launched in their careers. But here they were, continuing as students, asking what might be the best investment for their accumulated savings. I generally refer these couples to competent people in Christian stewardship professions. Many helpful and objective counselors are available for assistance without fee; however, some counselors are unethical.

How does a family manage its financial affairs to the glory of God? First, by setting aside a tithe. The tithe is to be treated with care and a sense of responsibility. Hopefully, one is pleased with his church and its program of worship, local services, biblical education, evangelism, outreach and world missions. If so, the Christian family may devote all or nearly all of their tithe to the local church and church institutions. Certainly, many secular institutions are also deserving of support. But the Christian should find other means than his tithe to meet these needs.

If there is a Christian cause that deserves support but is unrelated to the local church, the church will generally transfer contributions to it upon request. There are compelling reasons for making donations through a local church. A minister or someone on the church board or staff would be likely to know which organizations are worthy and which are not.

Furthermore, personal giving to an individual is not likely to be accepted as a deductible item on income taxes, even though the individual is engaged in missionary work. But that same gift channeled through a church is probably tax deductible. On the other hand, there are times when a tax benefit may be deliberately sacrificed when the purpose is worthy of support but is not technically tax exempt. Needs are not always tailored to government requirements or privileges.

A person may wish to give to an individual or a project even though his church is not in sympathy with the work to be supported. If one's church does not utilize resources with careful stewardship and biblical direction, nor provide the service of transferring funds to persons and projects of interest to donors, then the donation may be given directly. Numerous independent Christian organizations are doing superior work and deserve support. However, it is well known that many Christians are responsive to religious charlatans. The problem is significant to the degree that local and national governments are legislating to control abuses. It is not likely that they will stop all unethical appeals.

Why We Need to Give

It is important to recognize that there is a basic human need to give. If that need has been sublimated by selfishness, greed or neglect, the individual is reduced in his ability to function as a sensitive, enlightened human being. I am a better man when I give away some of that which God provides. The apostle Paul, in 2 Corinthians, argues for equalizing through giving—a voluntary means for correcting any inequities (2 Cor. 8—9).

The tithe was not instituted as a clever means by which religious leaders perpetuate their interests. If I believed that, I might give a tithe to charitable institutions that serve the needs of mankind, rather than to the church. Some people try to escape their spiritual duty by rationalizing away the origin of the church tithing principle. But to be full persons, whole persons, they need to give. And God has provided the tithe as a basic formula to assure the fulfillment of my need. It is as good a way as may be found to meet our human need to give. Giving is in the nature of things, in God and the universe. One should wish to fulfill his part in that natural order.

Reference has already been made to stewardship counselors. Most church denominations have developed stewardship offices to assist their members in the management of some of their financial affairs. For the most part, the counselors in these programs are deeply committed to the persons with whom they are counseling. Generally, they are excellent advisors. They begin by urging persons to write a will. Once estate protection has been established, there is time for a more leisurely approach to other aspects of financial planning. A number of instruments such as trusts and annuities may be explained and made available.

Often the stewardship counselor can show an interested party how he may donate to church or charitable service, save on income taxes, increase his security and end up with more money in his estate than if he did not contribute at all. At the present time, the laws of the land are constructed to provide tax shelters for those who practice careful stewardship. There is considerable debate over the appropriateness of some of these shelters and there will likely be changes in future laws regarding estate taxes.

Why We Need to Save
Ten percent of one's income should be set aside for

savings. Most young families do not save in a methodical way, and that which they do save is often eroded by purposeless spending.

There are excellent reasons for saving in a disciplined way. For example, a family who saves may be able to accumulate sufficient funds and free themselves from common limitations on their goals and desires. If they wish to move to another state or city, to change jobs, to educate their children, to purchase a luxury, they may do so with minimal concern. The independence afforded to a person with savings, the relief from fear of changing economic conditions, and the sense that one is "getting ahead" are other forceful arguments for saving money. Saving money is part of good stewardship, and it creates a sense of well-being in the savers.

A danger in saving is the possibility that one will become miserly and money will become an end in itself. Some persons unnecessarily go over and over personal bank balances, with which they are already very familiar. A person might become like Scrooge and "beguile the evening with his banker's books."

To avoid this danger, a family or an individual should save with purpose: to buy this or that when money accumulation permits, to give to a special project, to develop a hedge against emergency, to educate children or grandchildren, to plan retirement, and the like. Saving with a purpose prevents a man or woman from becoming materialistic or miserly. Once he has accumulated two or three thousand dollars in a bank account, a person without purpose is tempted to hoard money for its own sake.

Men and women may become attached to their savings to the degree that they cannot permit themselves to carry out their own worthy projects, such as financing the education of their children. Some parents are well able to assist their hard-working children to pay heavy college expenses, but the fund built for that very purpose has become too important to them. They cannot give it up.

Other men or women keep their families in penury when they have the financial resources to make the members more comfortable. They often attach some religious rationalization to their own miserliness. Sometimes they are able to maintain their spartan pattern because they are consistent in their own behavior. Like the apostle Paul they are comfortable in "suffering want," but uncomfortable when they "abound."

A Plan for Saving

Formulas may be designed to maximize savings. The following plan is a basic approach to be considered as a matter of Christian stewardship. A three- to six-months' salary equivalent ought to be kept in a local bank or savings and loan association earning interest. This should be in the type of account where it is available for immediate use. Insurance ought to be purchased at the time of marriage in an amount not less than $10,000. As soon as possible, in this latter part of the twentieth century, this should be raised to $100,000. When the insured is young, his premium payments are low, and dividends may be drawn in emergencies or used to help pay premiums. The first three years of an insurance policy may be the most difficult to finance. After that period the accumulations in the policy may be relied upon, if required, to pay a significant share of the premium.

A small amount may be put into an investment plan each month. Some investment clubs are formed by friends who place as little as $10 monthly into their mutual holdings. The members determine the stocks and bonds to be bought or sold. A portfolio develops. The participation is great fun if the transactions are carefully done and if the members do not permit the rise and fall of their spirits to be determined by the daily tapes from Wall Street or Toronto. If they do become "possessed" by the stock market, they should avoid participation and should transfer their savings to another kind of program.

There are other ways of managing savings that relate to larger Christian purposes. Couples may put some savings in bonds and annuities sold by Christian organizations they decide to support. If such an investment is lost, they should be gratified that it was used in a cause they favored. They should treat the loss as a donation and close the matter. For example, my wife and I invested a small amount in a Christian retirement center. If it should fail or stop dividend payments, we would not be offended. The purpose was worthy and the risk appropriate. Money is not so important to us that we must have absolute guarantee on its safety, though we do try to exercise reasonable prudence.

Another aspect of Christian family stewardship, already referred to, is the writing of a will. Despite the fact that a small army of money counselors, development men, attorneys, charitable organizations, government workers, and others barrage the population with the importance of making wills, more than half the population have not done so. Even professional money managers are often derelict in their personal affairs. The making of a will is simple and inexpensive, and it guarantees that an estate will be conserved for purposes valued by the owner before his death. If he does not direct distribution, the state will. Generally, the cost of dispersing assets to the government and the estate is relatively high in such an instance.

A Plan for Spending

Eighty percent of an income ought to provide the necessities of everyday living.[1] To live in that boundary requires careful planning, especially at the beginning. Many persons, principally women without husbands, who have the duty to stretch available money to meet the needs of their families, exhibit amazing abilities to remain solvent despite minuscule incomes. Middle-class families often have more trouble balancing their budgets than lower middle-class or poor families. And some women who live at poverty level are making ends meet. Students can thrive on a pittance without taking on ragged appearances. The amount one earns does not determine whether or not he will have personal monetary problems. How he spends his money does.

Setting up a budget is the most basic technique for family money management. The division of income for planned and controlled outgo is a budget. Persons who are not used to budget planning should begin by carefully listing what they actually spend for necessities and other goods and services over a period of time. Almost invariably, as is true when we analyze the use of our time, we are surprised to discover how much waste there is in unmanaged financial affairs. Only by a careful study may a couple be sure where overspending or underspending is taking place.

The American Bankers Association periodically publishes percentage figures that may be used as guidelines for family planning.[2] The figures change with social circumstances. For example, referring to the needs of the 1970s the A.B.A. reduced the recommended amount of savings a family should hold in emergencies to an equivalent of two months' income (down from three months'). The reduction was recommended because of the widespread application of private and public insur-

173

ance and medical programs to the population. Because of the rise in taxes and interest costs, the A.B.A. suggested that during this decade a family would be well advised to purchase a home costing less than two and a half times the annual income of the family. Other sources recommend that families may effectively defy the averages by living in towns and cities where costs are significantly lower than in others. Housing and tax costs may be double in one city what they are in another.

There are several warning signals that show if a couple is planning poorly. If a budget plan counts on extra income (such as a bonus or an expected raise), the plan is shaky. Anticipated increases are likely to become disappointments. Increments do not always arrive, inflation is a hidden tax, and costly unbudgeted emergencies occur as often as good fortune.

Another signal flashes when percentages get out of balance. For example, if loan or monthly payments (except for home, home improvements and automobile) rise to 20 percent of income, the couple may expect to be in serious financial difficulty. The national average for monthly credit payments is 14 or 15 percent. If 20 percent of one year's income would not pay the principal of all bills represented by monthly payments, excepting home and auto, then the family is likely overspending. In addition, reasons for increasing or incurring debts must be examined carefully. The replacement of a faulty water heater is almost always justified; a two-year loan for a vacation seldom is.

An important but little used technique for controlling a family budget is to plan ahead for five or ten years.[3] It is possible to do so effectively. In long-range planning a couple tries to visualize large expenditures, such as roofing the house, purchasing a car, or educating the children. These projections provide goals for above average saving, and saving for such projects protects families from ferocious interest costs.

Staying Out of Debt

The difference between a solvent family and an insolvent one may often be seen in the cost of servicing their debts. Rather than focusing on the amount of debts, persons ought to become interest-conscious and think in terms of interest paid and interest earned. One surely would prefer to collect it than to pay it. How to earn rather than pay interest is a gratifying lesson to learn at the beginning of marriage.

Perhaps a pleasant conclusion to the matter of family money management is to affirm the joys of a debt-free existence. So few families live with freedom from debt that most do not even think of it as an option. If each family were able to live for one year without the pressure of unnecessary indebtedness, it is not likely that they would again fall easily into the trap of purchasing luxuries, buying on impulse or using credit cards extensively.

A minister acquaintance of mine, now retired, decided to keep his first automobile until it was fully paid off and he had saved half of the cost of a new one. He then purchased a car at low monthly payments. Then by applying the same formula during the life of the second car, he was able to pay cash plus trade-in for the third car. He never again paid interest on the purchase of an automobile. He made monthly "car payments" to his bank account. In addition he earned interest on those savings, further forcing down the ultimate cost. It was a habit he maintained until his retirement. One could find no better example of discipline in the management of personal financial affairs.

Families ought to try some of these creative ways of

staying out of debt. They will like what they find. Relief from pressure, change in energy commitments, awareness of freedom, and meaning in stewardship are a few of the by-products of debt-free living.

Notes

1. George M. Bowman, *Here's How to Succeed with Your Money* (Chicago: Moody Press, 1960). This Toronto investment counselor argued for a 10-70-20 formula. My own formula was used by my family for some years before Bowman's program came to my attention. His treatment of the issues of money and family is recommended reading.
2. Brochure, by Family Concern, Inc., Wheaton, Illinois. This company makes easily available: (a) Money Management Library, (b) Teaching Your Child the Fiscal Facts of Life, and (c) Family Finance Packet.
3. "A Five-Year Plan for Managing Your Money," *Reader's Digest* (February 1974), p. 128ff. Summarized from an article in *Changing Times, The Kiplinger Magazine,* October, 1973.

PART SIX

MATURITY

Abraham came to mourn for Sarah, and to weep for her. (Gen. 23:2)

CHAPTER TWELVE

LONG MARRIAGE AND LONG LIFE— HAPPY COMPANIONS

Key points in this chapter include:
- why longtime marriages fail
- how boredom erodes marriage
- why talk, talk, talk is important

But speak thou the things which become sound doctrine: that the aged men be sober, grave, temperate, sound in faith, in charity, in patience. The aged women likewise, that they be in behavior as becometh holiness, not false accusers, not given to much wine, teachers of good things; that they may teach the young women to be sober, to love their husbands, to love their children, to be discreet, chaste, keepers at home, good, obedient to their own husbands, that the word of God be not blasphemed. (Titus 2:1-5)

The Mature Marriage

In the United States at present one in four divorces occurs in a marriage that is more than 15 years old. This fact is displacing the long-held belief that if a husband and wife invest many years in their relationship, solutions to their marital tensions are guaranteed. Why is it that so many longtime marriages fail?

Marriages require continuous attention, repair, change, and shifts in direction or order to achieve goals. Like launched rockets searching for their destination, marriages require "mid-course correction." In space exploration, corrections must be made because many problems and influences related to flight cannot be anticipated at the outset of the venture. Ongoing marriages require similar attention. New goals, or change and adjustment in primary goals, may be necessary. Fresh relationships with one's mate need to be developed on a regular and continuing basis.

For example, husband and wife may need to become reacquainted 15 or 20 years after the wedding. Heavy workloads in professional life and the rearing of children may have stifled their relationship. A man may sacrifice intimate time with his wife during vital years in order to invest more hours each week in his work. His business may have prospered while his marriage withered. And a wife may be preoccupied with child-rearing. After their children leave home or when professional life ends, the man and wife may find themselves unable or unwilling to renew their relationship, incapable of making mid-course corrections. They may feel they have nothing left on which to base their marriage. Loneliness and tension often follow—perhaps divorce.

Despite these doubts and frustrations, fantasies persist. Idealism is stubborn. Persons believe themselves to be realists, but their fantasy expectations—even demands—for perfect marriages make them unrealistic. They feel they ought to be able to enjoy an ideal marriage without the investment of a great deal of effort to improve personal relationships. They, therefore, dwell upon failures and disappointments. They distort human experience by overemphasizing problems and disregarding solutions. These exaggerated problems are seen to be inadequate fulfillment of youthful dreams and hopes. Some of these dreams grow out of fantasies imposed by their wishful or naive parents and idealistic religious leaders. Others are conferred by the young romantics themselves, starry-eyed lovers, magnifying intimate pleasures into unrealistic expectations. When the mythology does not hold up, marriage is blamed.

Even after long experience, many persons continue to hold onto their naive concepts and life problems. During recent years, Westerners, especially Americans, seem less sensible about what marriage is and what it can be. Divorce proceedings show that men and women presume that marriage should be perfect in intimacy, communication, companionship, security, family, and a solution to personal failure. Actually, marriage presents an opportunity to assist each other and children to meet needs, to encounter human problems—even tragedy—and carry burdens together.

Marriage between imperfect persons is forced to absorb the imperfections of those persons, and many reject or deprecate the institution itself as a result. The population in general little realizes what great expectations it has placed on marriage.[1] This makes one wonder whether our generation will be able to give up its fantasy in favor of practical reality.

Facing a New Set of Problems

The purpose of this chapter is to deal with several common problems faced by couples in later life when their children are launched. In many families, couples live their last 25 or more years together in an atmosphere shorn of romance, of dynamic, of joy, of conversation, of discovery.

Older Christian couples seem to fare better than non-Christians. This is sometimes due to a resignation in which Christians submit to present disappointments in order to attain heaven's reward. Even though real-life problems are sometimes unsolved for such Christian couples, their Christian "stoicism" may anesthetize them against some of the pain caused by those problems.

Difficulties common to the autumn of marriage have been catalogued many times. The various lists are similar. Wayne Dehoney prepared a chapter, "Warming the Empty Nest," for the symposium *The Marriage Affair.* Dehoney cited Clifford Adams' list of danger signals that indicate trouble for mates whose children have departed from home. The list includes: poor communication, declining compatibility, increasing inability to compromise, lack of cooperation, increasing selfishness, chronic criticism or nagging, neglect or indifference, and escapist behavior (such as "loner" activities, a one-person hobby, excessive viewing of television, or falling into gambling and drinking).[2] Only a few of these subjects will be reviewed in this chapter. All are deserving of development, but space limits this writing to only a few erosions of mature marriages. Boredom and communication failure will be reviewed in this chapter. Failing health, longer life, change and creative ways for meeting these issues will be suggested in the next and final chapter.

Boredom Erodes Marriages

Boredom is cumulative in a marriage. It builds up imperceptibly.

Our forefathers appear to have been more realistic than modern Americans. They did not believe that all of life had to progress smoothly. Many believed that some hardship improved their lives for they were conscious of their sinfulness. They needed "purging." Perhaps trouble in the world was good for man's soul. It prepared the race for heaven. Illness, poverty, grinding labor, disappointment and death were integral to life, requiring resignation. Most persons accepted their lot and prayed or hoped for improvement. Many recorded their feelings in poignant diary statements, telling about how ordeals drew husband, wife and children, as well as neighbors, together.

In family Bibles our resigned forebears listed their family's births and deaths. To insure the ongoing of their favorite name, sensitive parents sometimes gave succeeding children the same Christian name as that given to children who did not survive. Sometimes three or four consecutive newborns were given the name John, for example, by a hopeful mother until finally one survived. In one European family 17 children were born and died without surviving infancy. The eighteenth lived and became a celebrity, Enrico Caruso.

But human resignation has all but disappeared. No one wants to return to the harsh way of living that stopped the breath of infants. Yet we should know from observation that life is not soft. To keep a zest for life, one must be able and willing to take his share of buffeting, of disappointment, even tragedy. Boredom is a continuous, low-key kind of buffeting which one must often bear. It is integral to orderly life.

Boredom in later life is, in part, the result of unsatisfactory early life. No reading, no hobbies, no friends in early and middle years mean no interest in books, hobbies, or friends in later life. It is well to remember that we are, when we are old, what we were when we were young, only more so. A dissatisfied old man was likely a dissatisfied young man. And generous, loving elders were probably virtuous in love and generosity in their youth. Aging processes accent both the best and worst in an individual.

Boredom may intensify for an individual when he fantasizes about the past. By comparison to what preceded, present activity may appear undramatic and unsatisfactory to an unhappy person. Young marrieds, absent from their comfortable paternal home and struggling to form their own families, may romanticize their former circumstances. They compare unfavorably their present situation with what they remember of their previous life. It is a way of escaping from their present difficult or tense lives. But when fantasy passes, as surely it will, the sublimated boredom reasserts itself and is accentuated.

Many middle-aged persons find boredom very difficult to overcome. Aging generally brings with it rigidity or unwillingness to change. As a result, new programming for life experiences all but ceases in the middle years for many persons. Patterns have been set. The individual tends to function on the residue of his productive earlier years. He perceives experiences as threatening, and fear looms more quickly than before. Fear of change—even fear of the future—weakens the will to face new and dynamic experiences. Where this attitude prevails, boredom with present circumstances and fear of change mingle to create unhappiness.

Is There a Cure?

Boredom can be alleviated; but a good deal of effort must be expended to succeed. It is exasperating to counselors that many persons do not generate the will to solve their problems. Counseling sessions often fail for lack of counselee participation. Participants seem to be lethargic and counseling becomes wasted effort. Participation, including homework, is necessary if sessions are to achieve their purposes. Rather than attempting to solve their problems, counselees often appear to be searching for better reasons to justify what they have already decided to do in their marriages—to call it "quits" or to live in a tenuous truce with their mates.

Bored partners should return to an affirmative approach toward each other. An older married couple, casting about for reinforcement of romance, should recall and do some of the things that were enjoyable at the beginning of the relationship. The well-known principle of psychologist William James may apply: "Feelings follow actions." James cited the illustration of a man in the woods confronted by a bear. The man turned from the animal and ran to safety. In the security of his cabin he began trembling. The memory of the bear and of his running to escape caused the emotion of fear to arise, and the man trembled. Had a strong feeling of fear overcome him in the presence of the bear, he would have frozen on the spot and been mauled by the bear. The fact that his action (running) came before his feeling (trembling with fear) saved his life. A belief in the principle of acting before feeling may be helpful in many areas of life.

As a principle, a person should learn to act as he would *if* he possessed the desired emotion. After the right action is taken the emotion will follow. How this may apply in a marriage is suggested by one writer: "Open the car door for your wife, kiss her again; rub his neck; do whatever is necessary to revive early feelings for one another."[3] It may be that old emotions will revive and bloom once more.

Married partners may be able to arouse former affection by experimenting with various experiences of touching. The effort has been productive for many. A man and wife should force themselves to hold hands again, if they have ceased the practice. The act may arouse initial negative or self-conscious responses, but the change in behavior may in time change attitudes. It is not easy to argue or find fault with a person with whom one is holding hands.

The Value of Variety

Variety invigorates. However, it requires imagination, energy and liberation to overpower boredom with variety. Each member of a marriage should fulfill various sub-roles in his or her relationship with the other. My wife is to me a housekeeper, a co-worker, a companion, a mistress, a mother figure, a friend, a counselor, even a foil in a joke. She responds as she senses my mood. The result is that she is always interesting to me. If her own actions and words are true, as I believe they are, I, as her husband, fulfill several sub-roles in her life: provider, lover, confidant, father figure, repairman, and friend.

As a marriage matures, the variety of roles should be maintained and enriched. This will be difficult in marriages in which mate rivalry becomes strong. As women develop their own lives and careers they sometimes enter into competition with their husbands for professional recognition, salary levels, and social participation. The phenomenon of dual careers is a relatively recent development. While it does add pressures to a marriage, it also promises the possibility of richer, more varied relationships. Society has yet to discover what mutuality in professional careers can do for marriages.

Each marriage partner should remain open to growth —mental, spiritual, social. Each should assist the other in meeting his or her needs which, when met, reinforce the personhood of both. Each should surrender some things; each should incorporate some things. These should be enthusiastic, conscious actions, giving out and taking in.

During our marriage I have sublimated some of my interests in sports; my wife has increased her interest in travel. We found that after we had launched our children into adult life we had to make other changes and shifts. No longer did we devote our evenings to children and their needs. Schedules changed. More money became available for our personal and stewardship interests. We had more private time together. Grandchildren introduced an unexpected inspiration to renew ourselves for participation with youngsters. We became aware that we were to be wise and helpful, but not so authoritative with our adult children as we were when they were young. Energy levels declined somewhat, and adaptations had to be made for differentials between my wife and me. Emerging health problems for her forced us into diet changes.

It is an old cliché and truism that no one is too old to learn or try something new. Each mate, then, must strive to develop variety in the way he relates in his marriage, so that boredom will not have a chance to dominate.

In counseling sessions one discovers that unhappy persons tend to set up rigid patterns of action. Ultimately, they fall into slavish repetitions and regard deviations from the patterns as nearly immoral. For example, the intimate marriage act may become strictly scheduled, rather than developing spontaneously. It may follow a rigid and predictable pattern from initiation to completion. No changes, no experimentation, no fresh communication, and no real awareness occur. And the couple is surprised that boredom has overcome the relationship. Even some young couples complain of boredom in their sexual intimacy. How can slavishly repeated activity be anything but monotonous?

Poor Communication Erodes Marriage

During the years of a marriage it is common for mates to fall into psychological deafness and sullen silence. Like many other problems, communication decline is imperceptible at the beginning. During early marriage, subtle barriers build up. Sharing of ideas and activities declines, and may disappear. Only alert couples will avoid dilution or loss of their own communication.

Communication effectiveness with work associates and friends is no guarantee that one will maintain open communication with his mate. It is common for one mate to develop socially, spiritually or intellectually more than the other. Great differences in these areas were more acceptable a generation ago than they are presently. Women were expected to be basically domestic. Albert Einstein could be happily married to a simple, peasant-like woman, but it is less likely for a similar marriage to be successful today. There is an expectation that husband and wife should maintain a level of nearly equal sophistication.

A happy early marriage is no assurance of a meaningful relationship in later years. Sturdy things grow weak, unless something is done to prevent deterioration. A couple who has been married for many years is often perplexed about any loss of first love. Husband and wife ask themselves, "Where did we go wrong? When did it happen?" Erosion may have occurred because no effort was expended to maintain the relationship. When repairs were needed, the marriage was expected to fix itself. Marriages seldom do.

Several marriages recorded in the Old Testament began on a high plane and with great promise, but later encountered hard times. We read, "Abraham loved her." The long romance of Abraham and Sarah is a classic. Years later their son Isaac married Rebekah: "And Isaac brought her into his mother Sarah's tent, and took Rebekah, and she became his wife; and he loved her: and Isaac was comforted after his mother's death." And we know that Jacob was willing to be indentured to gain the hand of Rachel: "And Jacob served seven years for Rachel; and they seemed unto him but a few days, for the love he had to her." Despite these genuine love stories the marriages later ran into difficulties. They were tested with problems that today would destroy them. The patriarchs were more realistic than we are about the world and about human nature. They did not dissolve their marriages when difficult times came. They prevailed over the problems. Sometimes they solved them; sometimes they simply rode them out. Where in the Scriptures does one find divorce or abandonment by persons who loved God?

Reading the full biblical accounts impresses one that communication, or lack of it, had much to do with family success or failure. An analysis of the conversations in the Bible, between husbands and wives, between parents and children, is a worthy exercise. For instance, the writer of 1 Kings accounted for the unsatisfactory conduct of Adonijah as the result of communication failure between David and his son: "And his father had not displeased him at any time in saying, Why hast thou done so?" (1 Kings 1:6). There apparently was so little communication between them that David was not able to correct Adonijah when it was necessary. With his family generally David appears to have been a poor disciplinarian. He loved his family members deeply but not well.

Even in our present communication-conscious age, it has been discovered that some mothers devote as little as 15 minutes a day to meaningful communication with their preschoolers.[4] And one family study cited by the Christian Medical Association shows that, after a year of marriage, the average couple spends about 37 minutes a week in exclusive conversation.[5] Older married couples may feel the need of increased communication with their mates but they have had little practice for it in their earlier years.

Talk, Talk, Talk!

If communication was ever present in a marriage and declined, it is usually possible to reinstate it. Counselors have developed several easily utilized systems. One such technique begins with husband and wife sitting and facing each other. A removable shield is placed between them, preventing visual contact for at least a portion of the verbal exchange. The husband and wife are thus limited in the nonverbal responses they can receive from each other. A third person is sometimes used, and sometimes a fourth in order to provide both male and female observer-counselors. They assist by encouraging the troubled couple to talk out differences. The observers may raise questions, moderate conflicts and serve as facilitators in various ways. Sometimes the equipment is rigged with approval and disapproval lights controlled by the participants so that no other parties are required.[6]

A similar but simplified type of game can be devised, without either paraphernalia or third parties, so that husband and wife may talk to each other and gain feedback. Face to face, they are given equal time slots in which to cover specific concerns, and an ending time is set. The couple is encouraged to treat problems slowly and with care.

It is well known that marriage partners who freely talk to each other are more likely to have happy and stable marriages. As talk decreases, the possibility of dissolution increases.[7]

One research study concluded that many happy marriages found nonverbal communication to be particularly effective. Little verbal language was used between these mates for lengthy periods. Elements of this study seem to contradict the general attitude among researchers that the greater the verbalization, the greater the chance for happiness. Apparently, the age of the marriage, the common interests of the mates, and the warmth of understanding related to a love relationship may make nonverbal communication more effective and satisfying than verbal for some couples.

The way leisure time is spent by man and wife, and how much of that time is spent in conversation together, affect the happiness of a marriage. In a study that included 11 countries, it was discovered that the average leisure time spent by husband and wife together was 2.1 to 4.3 hours a day.[8] It was found that the greater the amount of time spent together, the stronger the marriage. The best use of leisure time for building marriage solidarity is conversation. Mates who talk tend to inform each other of their own activities in which the partners do not share. In this way, separate interests become mutual. Researchers believe that the way to save a marriage is to talk, talk, talk!

Notes

1. Article, *Presbyterian Life*, January 1, 1970, p. 20.
2. J. Allan Petersen, ed. *The Marriage Affair* (Wheaton: Tyndale House,), p. 403.
3. Article, *Presbyterian Life*, March 1, 1970, p. 20.
4. "Who's Raising the Kids?" *Newsweek* (September 22, 1975), p. 55.
5. *Christian Family Ministries*, May 1976. Wheaton, Illinois.
6. Mary Jo Takach, " 'Sam,' the Flashing Marriage Counselor," *San Francisco Examiner*, April 30, 1972, *This World*.
7. Joseph Fabry, "Keep Talking—You May Save Your Marriage," *San Francisco Examiner*, May 23, 1971, p. 20.
8. Ibid.

CHAPTER THIRTEEN

A PHOTO FINISH— BOTH WINNERS

Key points in this chapter include:
- how increasing life span affects marriages
- how change threatens happiness for senior adults
- how to accept passing years
- when a sense of humor can save a marriage
- why sex is important in mature marriages
- how to stay happy—10 practical steps

And Sarah was an hundred and seven and twenty years old: these were the years of the life of Sarah. And Sarah died in Kirjath-arba; the same is Hebron in the land of Canaan: and Abraham came to mourn for Sarah, and to weep for her. . . . And Abraham stood up, and bowed himself to the people of the land, even to the children of Heth. And he communed with them, saying, If it be your mind that I should bury my dead out of my sight; hear me, and entreat for me to Ephron the son of Zohar, that he may give me the cave of Machpelah, which he hath, which is in the end of his field; for as much money as it is worth he shall give it me for a possession of a buryingplace amongst you. . . . And Ephron answered Abraham, saying unto him, My Lord, hearken unto me: the land is worth four hundred shekels of silver; what is that betwixt me and thee? Bury therefore thy dead. And Abraham hearkened unto Ephron; and Abraham weighed to Ephron the silver, which he had named in the audience of the sons of Heth, four hundred shekels of silver, current money with the merchant. And the field of Ephron, which was in Machpelah, which was before Mamre, the field, and the cave which was therein, and all the trees that were in the field, that were in all the borders round about, were made sure unto Abraham for a possession in the presence of the children of Heth, before all that went in at the gate of his city. And after this, Abraham buried Sarah his wife in the cave of the field of Machpelah before

Mamre: the same is Hebron in the land of
Canaan. (Gen. 23:1,2,7-9,14-19)

Shakespeare, in "As You Like It," described the
physical ages of men:

All the world's a stage,
And all the men and women merely players;
They have their exits and their entrances;
And one man in his time plays many parts,
His acts being seven ages. At first the infant,
Mewling and puking in the nurse's arms;
Then the whining school-boy, with his satchel
And shining morning face, creeping like snail
Unwillingly to school. And then the lover,
Sighing like furnace, with a woeful ballad
Made to his mistress' eyebrow. Then a soldier
Full of strange oaths, and bearded like the pard,
Jealous in honour, sudden and quick in quarrel,
Seeking the bubble reputation
Even in the cannon's mouth. And then the justice,
In fair round belly with good capon lin'd,
With eyes severe and beard of formal cut,
Full of wise saws and modern instances;
And so he plays his part. The sixth age shifts
Into the lean and slipper'd pantaloon,
With spectacles on nose and pouch on side;
His youthful hose, well sav'd, a world too wide
For his shrunk shank; and his big manly voice,
Turning again toward childish treble, pipes
And whistles in his sound. Last scene of all,
That ends this strange eventful history,
In second childishness and mere oblivion;
Sans teeth, sans eyes, sans taste, sans everything.

Shakespeare's seven ages of man are, in our era, reduced to five. From infancy to childhood, from child-

hood to puberty, and from puberty to adulthood—these are the first three periods. None of these is discussed in detail here, but each significantly influences the last two periods. Puberty years especially affect the attitudes and conduct of the final decades of one's life.

The fourth age brings a person from adulthood to late middle age. The tensions of old age begin to appear in the latter part of this highly productive period. During this time-frame a marriage confronts new challenges. Robert Lee blames some of the problems of a mature marriage on middle age itself. He writes that the middle-aged have "the general uneasiness of being in the afternoon of life."[1] Many persons in this period of life never learn to cope with the fact of inevitable decline and death—either theirs or their partner's. If one mate declines markedly in health, the other may find the change hard to accept. Intimacy may stop, duties are neglected, and suspicions are voiced. One partner may withdraw entirely.

The final period follows the transition from middle age to old age. In societies like those found in the United States and Canada, oriented in the current century toward a youth culture, there is an onus to growing old. Formerly, authority and honor were automatically afforded the aged. This may have been excessive, but current attempts to weaken the influence of elders seem to be self-defeating. A society needs the wisdom and participation of elders. And elders need to participate in order to maintain their self-esteem. Unfortunately, some elders isolate themselves and complain about their lot, blaming others for their isolation.

There must be better ways than our society has found to provide appropriate environment for seniors. One health school's approach is for elders to refuse to be put down and refuse to put themselves down.[2] Studies of seniors show that they are happier, in better health, and more involved than is commonly believed. Nevertheless, much improvement is needed to discover the place in society for elders. They need a better press and increased opportunities to participate.

Intergeneration tensions are not limited to those between seniors and younger people. There is much that needs to be done to create better understanding between generations on every level. Polarization of these various groups may be one of the worst blunders of modern society. Ill will has developed because of the creation of false centers of loyalty related to peer interests. A person ought not to be considered worthy simply because he happens to be in a favored age group; nor should he be shown disrespect because his age group is out of favor.

Old Age—a Growing Challenge

Old age is more of a problem in recent times than it was earlier. Before the current century, old men hobbling along village walks were only a small segment of the community. The average age at which a person died was only a few years beyond the time of child-bearing.

The median age in the population at the founding of the United States was less than 16 years. In 1976, 200 years later, it was about 29 years, nearly double. When Lincoln delivered his farewell address to the people of Springfield in 1861, he spoke of himself as an old man. He was 52 years of age. At the turn of the century the average marriage lasted 20 or so years, until the death of one of the mates. Today a marriage of 50 years is common.[3]

The increased length of marriages creates new problems for couples and society. There is no precedent in the history of society that will help modern couples know what to do with their own relationships for many years after their children leave home. Almost all parents are gratified to have their children launched into adult experience, into their own homes and careers. They look forward to privacy and independence in their later years. Yet, many find their new life accompanied by a hollowness, an emptiness. The marital problems that husbands and wives encounter in this period are not so much related to the absence of their children as it is to finding or rediscovering one another in a new exclusive relationship. Older married couples are not concerned with the absence of children as much as with the absence of purpose.

As persons grow older, previous concerns become exaggerated—health, financial security, boredom, activities, and the like. Health problems are a special preoccupation of the aged. In the end, each person must die of something. Historically, accident, childbirth, and disease took many individuals before they reached old age. With improved safety techniques and medical services, the natural deterioration of the body became the major threat to life and happiness. Men and women who survive to old age generally experience debilitating physical deterioration. The study of the aged and their declining health, geriatrics, has become a major division of medicine.

Other problems add their share to the burden of old age. Economics are a constant concern, especially when inflation mushrooms. The decline of earning and purchasing power becomes increasingly evident. Additional frustration comes from the fact that younger generations appear to shoulder aside, without empathy, their seniors. Denied the satisfaction of meaningful involvement in society, elders are left with a way of life over which they have, or feel they have, little control.

So this last period of married life, from the time the last child leaves home until the death of one partner, has increased in length. In many cases it is the longest period of a marriage. Yet, it has not received enough attention by researchers or forethought by married couples.

It is often assumed that because a man and wife have maintained their marriage relationship to this last time-frame in their experience, all is well. The assumption, of course, is often erroneous. There are enough resources available to offer important assistance to all marriages, including long-established ones. Many need repair and deserve fair attention to increase their effectiveness, their happiness.

In later years, persons tend to lose perspective. The length of time between their childhood and the current moment is perceived to be short. And they are forced to come to terms with the fact that the end of their life is rushing forward to meet them. Time has become a very precious thing to them, and they wish to drain something meaningful from whatever remains. This wish may become so intense that a person will sometimes sacrifice a lifetime of relationships by abandoning his home and reputation in the hope of finding elusive happiness. A man may leave his wife to marry a person less than half his age. He may abandon his religion, his work, his former friends. He probably will not survive long enough to build a new and satisfying life. Despair, even suicide, may follow as tragic consequences of his desperate break with his wife and family.

The Fear of Change

Changes are not generally welcome regardless of a person's age.[4] Habit holds men and women in the manner they do things and the way they act in relationships. One source argued, after making careful studies of several community situations, that change is threatening even when the specific change can be shown to be beneficial.[5] A person may pay lip service to the benefits of change and still resist it forcefully. And resistance to change tends to increase with age. The fear of change is one of the factors that causes some elders to resign themselves to death.

Some elders rationalize their decline in activity with unconvincing lists of their limitations as elders. Older persons should maintain their sexual intimacy in marriage, should befriend youthful persons, should do volunteer work in church or elsewhere, should discover meaningful projects for participation, should keep physically active, should enlarge their sense of humor, should cultivate prayer experiences, and should maintain a strong belief in the life of the mind and spirit even when threatened with physical decline. No one should resign from life because the time remaining to him is short.

A Mature Marriage Can Be Creative

There are practical things that older couples should consider as they face the closing decades of their lives. The following suggestions may be helpful in keeping their attitudes positive and healthy. If these purposes become part of a mature marriage, that marriage will continue to be creative into its later years.

1. *Accept the fact of the passing years.* This advice has been repeated by numerous professionals in marriage counseling. Although the inevitability of aging appears to be obvious, it is a matter of record that much of the population refuses to accept or adapt to time's movement. To escape the thought of aging, some oldsters attempt to emulate the young, or they become nostalgic about their own puberty experiences, or drown themselves in distractions, like alcoholism or collecting junk.

Longtime counselors are acquainted with examples of these efforts to escape.

Robert Browning wrote: "Grow old along with me! The best is yet to be. The last of life, for which the first was made." Browning and his wife Elizabeth lived most fully during the latter half of their lives. Browning insisted that God had a plan for a person's whole life. Youth is less than half of it. Brave men and women wish to see it all. The Brownings savored their married life more than they had earlier believed possible. The Brownings were not married until Elizabeth was 40 years of age. Their love for each other is classic. In her magnificent sonnets to her husband, Mrs. Browning asked, "How do I love thee?" She answered in her sublime poetry, closing her best known sonnet with the words: "And if God should choose, I shall love thee better after death." For her, death would be the last transition of her marriage—but only a transition, not an end. If one sees the afterlife as another period to be lived under God's guidance, he will be less likely to resign himself to old age and to death as final.

2. *Stay young in heart.* A part of remaining young is to be sure there is variety in life. Older people fall into the habit of always doing the same things in the same ways. Resisting this habit helps maintain a youthful spirit. We have earlier discussed how acting as one ought to act will generate a desired feeling. Acting in appropriate ways will likely arouse appropriate emotions, and these in turn will motivate continued action. Doing things makes persons *want* to do things. By this means boredom may be minimized.

Being young at heart has as much to do with actions as with attitudes. In fact, not all young people have a young-at-heart attitude. Some are antiquated at 21.

Marshall McLuhan identified old people in his analogy of automobile drivers. If a driver constantly cocks his eye toward the rear view mirror, he is concentrating on the past, that which he has already traversed. The young driver concentrates on the view from the windshield. The person who is young at heart, regardless of his age, does not look back in longing very often, does not stop growing mentally and spiritually, does not lose sense of the future, and does not disregard the value of tomorrow or the day after that.

One needs to remember that for children engaged in play, time stands still. Happy people are not concerned with time. Time seems to suspend itself for happy lovers in any period of their lives.[6]

3. *Keep useful and active.* In a study of a group of scientists it was shown that their professional production during their sixties and seventies remained at 65 percent to 80 percent of that of their fourth and fifth decades.[7] Such continued usefulness can be satisfying. Even after one lays down the tools of his profession he may engage in many meaningful and necessary enterprises. Having retired from his excellent job, a friend of mine became the lay leader of his church. He did everything he was asked to do, from reproducing bulletins to keeping treasurer's books. He avoided the possibility that he would become a troublesome old man by volunteering his services and doing only that which he was asked to do. Persons with that attitude are asked to do more and more things. They may have to learn to say no as well as yes.

4. *Play games that keep marriage dynamic.* For example, following is a simplified form of tests used by psychologists, recommended to married couples by Dr. Robert Lee. Husband and wife sit across from one another and each completes the sentence, "Our marriage would be better if ... " They alternate contributions.

The exchange may include several responses which should be followed up with analysis, but it is basically a self-help technique. A game of this nature should be helpful in achieving the mid-course correction discussed earlier. Such games have become an effective educational tool.[8] Why should they not be used to instruct and improve life for elders as they do for young students?

It is important that one should not confuse the right and wrong uses of games. Playing some "games" in marriage and the family can be destructive, as Eric Berne pointed out in his book *Games People Play.* Berne has been credited as one of the developers of Transactional Analysis. Thomas Harris has further developed this formula for analysis in his best-selling book, *I'm OK—You're OK.* Following Harris' or Berne's approach to the definition of games, most analysts would agree that games can be destructive. However, the educational game discussed above is a conscious effort agreed upon by all participants. The rules are determined in advance and dropping out is permitted. The games to which Harris and Berne refer are manipulative, superficial, and wrongly motivated.[9] They are not mutually beneficial.

5. *Plan to remarry each other on a wedding anniversary.* Arrangements should be made with the church and pastor. Flowers, simulated license and a reception should be included. The couple's children, even grandchildren, may participate. If possible, a second honeymoon should follow. The couple's adult children may be willing to finance the venture. Anyone who has met a couple on a second honeymoon cannot doubt the salutary effect it can have. Many couples testify to an intensification of affection and heightened sensitivity toward each other as the result of a ceremony of marriage renewal.

Although my wife and I have well passed our thirtieth anniversary, we have not arranged for public renewal of our vows. Perhaps we shall do so at some future anniversary. However, on that thirtieth anniversary our children arranged a major event, which included the gathering of the immediate family, a banquet, a program with recordings from absent friends, a few small gifts and one large one—a scholarship fund in our name for students at the college where I serve. No other gesture could have pleased us more. That anniversary became a major moment in our marriage.

6. *Maintain a strong, intimate physical relationship.* More than 30 years have passed since she became my bride. We remain intense lovers, sharing an intimacy that greatly surpasses our first love and passion. We have grown heavier and have taken on other common evidence of aging. Her hair is "salt and pepper," the lines have deepened, and the gait is not so energetic. But she remains to me the most beautiful thing I have ever seen. If God should permit, I certainly would choose to love her after death, as Elizabeth Browning hoped to love Robert. In any event, we shall not lose our attraction for each other in this life, and we will continue to express that attraction in our physical relationship.

It is good for children to know that their parents maintain active sexual interest in one another. Children commonly believe everyone in the world is sexually active except their parents. Because parents are hesitant to let them know about continued marital intimacy, children suspect that after the conception of their last brother or sister their mother and father have followed the path of chastity. The discovery that they have been incorrect in this belief may create distress for adolescents. Sometimes a young woman will seek counseling because she has stumbled upon her parents in private intimacy. She is surprised and shocked at the sexual relationships of her parents. She may sometimes apply sordid connotations to it. Usually, questioning will reveal that the daughter allows the sexual act as appropriate to any married couple except her parents.

When children are well along in elementary school they should become aware of their parents' sexual interest in one another. Gestures of affection between mother and father, their periodic retreats from the rest of the family—in these and other ways they instruct their children that sexual intimacy belongs to marriage. And they should learn that it is part of marriage even in the later years. Sex is seen as blatant and sleazy in much of modern life. If their parents keep their sexual intimacy a total secret, youths are forced to believe that no other environments exist for sex than the sordid or superficial ones that are widely publicized. They should sense the beauty of intimacy in their homes. Sex ought to be rescued from theaters, back seats of automobiles, bars, motel rooms, and the beds of prostitutes.

7. *Keep talking.* It has been noted earlier that communication may begin to decay at the outset of a marriage and continue an imperceptible decline during ensuing years. How is communication reinstated? The secret is to talk and listen, to listen and talk, as never before. One must consciously make an effort. Practice will increase communication skills. Topics can grow from reading, daily experience, family concerns or, most usefully, from questions one asks the other.

8. *Develop or keep a sense of humor.* Happy marriages enjoy humor. They experience laughter, and even smile away some cutting remarks or harsh attitudes. Humor can remind us that our own overly-sensitive natures are continually wounded by self-inflicted offenses. One mate may accuse the other of a deliberate

offense. But offenses are seldom deliberate. Anyone who understands human nature and its mechanisms will avoid the temptation to read sinister motives into every word or action. Accepting human nature, one should laugh at its foibles. Margie Casady wrote, "If you're active and savvy at 30, you'll be warm and witty at 70."[10]

One woman kidded her husband about his negative attitude. At first he took offense, but he ultimately praised her for resisting his dark spirit. Her humor was not a put-down, but a gentle shock treatment that prevented him from wallowing in negativism and worry. He saw, at last, that his own pessimism and sensitive nature were the culprits, not the people with whom he had been finding fault.

9. *Cultivate new as well as old friendships.* It has been found that strong marriages include, as primary, friendships that are discovered and cultivated by mates after their marriages. The couples that formed the happiest marriages tend to be those where husband and wife drop close ties with former friends identified with their single days. In mature marriages new friendships are important because they resist the tendency of older people to insulate themselves—insulate to such an extent that they sometimes become narrow and suspicious. Friendmakers tend to be open, accepting and cheerful. Certainly friendships of long standing should be maintained in church, at home, in social or business relationships. But a couple should mix these long-standing friends with new ones.

And older married couples should not neglect the children—their own adult children. Of course, parents should stay out of their adult children's personal affairs, respond only when invited on matters of counsel, and learn how to treat them as responsible adults. Parents ought to be willing to give them up to their own friendships and goals. They ought to know that unless a child leaves home, leaves the nest, they have failed in rearing that child. A clinging adult child is neither mature nor responsible. He is unprepared for the death of his parents. Happy is the parent who develops a mature friendship with his adult children. When parents and children are accepting friends, the job of parenting by the elders is completed.

Learn the marvels of celebration in friendship. Simply stated, celebration is reveling in the personal presence of those one loves. The one who celebrates is not concerned with yesterday or tomorrow, but with this moment and its beauty. Such celebrations of friendship are registered indelibly upon the participant's memory. The same principle may be applied in varying ways to many types of persons with whom one comes in contact. Celebration may even teach him to enjoy the presence of a person he may not like, or whose life patterns are contrary to his own. That kind of celebration may be tenuous and difficult at first, but it is possible.

10. *Spend more time refining spiritual relationships.* Because Christians see a spiritual significance to every aspect of their lives, marriage ought to especially focus on spiritual insight. Marriage ought to be consciously and deliberately spiritual. And if a person is sensitive, he will transfer that perception into meaningful action.

My wife's physician uncle retired at the close of World War II. Thereafter, as part of their relationship, aunt and uncle began the practice of reading through the Bible once a year. I recall visiting their home during the seventeenth reading. On an even later visit Uncle Doc was 95 years old, and still reading the Bible with his wife. At this writing he has passed his one-hundredth birthday. The couple has maintained a continuing enthusiasm for life because they have grown.

There are only a few general ways in which persons may relate to one another: socially, physically, culturally, professionally. The spiritual dimension ought to be part of all these relationships. Because of effects of aging, relationships that are strictly social, professional and physical must decline. Even most cultural interests fade. But a relationship that includes spiritual awareness may actually intensify as the years pass, especially if those spiritual interests have been alive since youth.

The spiritual dimension builds into marriages an ever-increasing awareness of eternal values. And if that is true, marriage is clearly a means by which men and women may express Christian virtues, growing in Christian graces throughout life. A marriage that has a sound spiritual basis will be creative in spite of the ravages of years.

Notes

1. Victoria Billings, "Middle Age—Marriage Crisis Time," *San Francisco Examiner* January 21, 1972, p. 22.
2. Associated Press report, *The Milwaukee Journal*, October 23, 1973. Lois Geraci Ernst was nearly overcome by the "youth-oriented society." She fought back and rose in her profession of advertising. In 1973 she resisted the common tendency to advertise that a product would make a woman look younger. She struck a national response with her slogan, "You're not getting older—you're getting better."
3. Robert Betts, "Marriage—How Its' Changing," *San Francisco Examiner*, January 9, 1972.
4. Mayers, Richards and Webber, *Reshaping Evangelical Higher Education* (Grand Rapids: Zondervan Publishing House, 1972), p. 88.
5. *American School and University*, June 1973, p. 28.
6. Marshall McLuhan, *The Medium Is the Massage* (New York: Bantam Books, Inc., 1967).
7. Ibid.
8. Mayers, Richards and Webber, *Reshaping Evangelical Higher Education*, p. 109, 110.
9. Thomas A. Harris, *I'm OK—You're OK* (New York; Harper & Row, Inc., 1967), p. 51.
10 Margie Casady, "If You're Active and Savvy at 30, You'll be Warm and Witty at 70," *Psychology Today* (November, 1975), p. 138.